sizzle

I dedicate **Sizzle** to all the wonderful people, mostly men, who have barbecued my breakfasts, brunches, lunches and dinners over the years, in particular my brother Colin and husband Remo who have both managed to channel their pyromaniacal tendencies to a very good end, and to my son Luca who learnt to cook on the barbecue, grilling, sizzling, frying and frizzling, and who is set to be the next King of the Campfire. Men and fire. Thanks for the food, the fun and the warmth!

sizzle

sensational barbecue food

Julie Biuso

Photography by Aaron McLean

NEW HOLLAND

acknowledgements

I've had a great team to help on this book. First, a big thank you to Belinda Cooke from New Holland for backing my idea and supporting me all the way through. Thanks also to Matt Turner from New Holland, and to Renée Lang for her companionship and good editing. I want to make a special acknowledgement to Christine Hansen for her gorgeous design. Thanks, as always, to Ray Richards, my literary agent. I had wonderful fun in the kitchen with Janya Chan, my assistant – it hardly seemed like work at all – and Aaron McLean, my photographer. Thanks for the terrific shots, Aaron, and to Julia Wyatt for doing a sterling job of propping. And it's great to have Yvonne Thynne back applying her considerable talents as a publicist. Finally, thanks to my family, especially Remo, Luca and Ilaria.

I'd like to acknowledge the following companies that helped with this book:

BBQ Factory
www.bbqfactory.co.nz
Ph 0800 800 836

Allium Interiors
Ph 09 524 4242

Eon Design Centre
Ph 09 368 4860

French Country Collections
For stockists phone 09 376 6440

Hancocks
For stockists phone 0800 699463

La Cigale
Ph 09 366 9361

Living & Giving
Ph 0800 548464

McPherson's
Wiltshire Bar-B-Mate
Ph 0800 655 269

Nest
Ph 09 361 5555

Romantique
Ph 09 360 9669

Superb Herbs
Ph 09 837 0500

The Fabric Room
Ph 09 366 1905

The Studio of Tableware
Ph 09 638 8082

First published in 2006 by New Holland Publishers (NZ) Ltd
Auckland • Sydney • London • Cape Town

www.newhollandpublishers.co.nz

218 Lake Road, Northcote, Auckland, New Zealand
14 Aquatic Drive, Frenchs Forest, NSW 2086, Australia
86–88 Edgware Road, London W2 2EA, United Kingdom
80 McKenzie Street, Cape Town 8001, South Africa

ISBN-13: 978 1 86966 117 5
ISBN-10: 1 86966 117 6

Managing editor: Matt Turner
Design: Christine Hansen
Editor: Renée Lang

A catalogue record for this book is available from the National Library of New Zealand

10 9 8 7 6 5 4 3 2 1

Colour reproduction by SC (Sang Choy) International Pte Ltd, Singapore
Printed by Tien Wah Press (Pte) Ltd

contents

introduction

When I was a kid we used to have fantastic all-day family picnics at the beach most Sundays throughout summer. We'd race each other there to get the best spot under the pohutukawa tree and set up camp. Lunch was usually shared sandwiches, salads, cold meats, bacon and egg pies and cakes, that sort of thing, and the afternoon was spent swimming, playing beach cricket or volleyball, or pretending to read a book; invariably the adults dozed off. Once the heat of the day died down, the barbecues came out. We were all envious of my brother-in-law Billy's barbecue. He had converted an old kerosene drum into a barbecue by cutting it in half and sticking it on metal legs. It had a mean heat and anything cooked on it smelled and tasted delicious. Those summers, with smoke in the air and the smell of sausages or steak sizzling on the grill, hold a special place in my heart. We had such fun. We wanted the summer to go on forever.

Nothing much has changed. Come summer, I see families gathering down the bottom of my street in Auckland's Little Shoal Bay, the kids running wild, the mother laying out a picnic while the father stands at the barbecue grilling and sizzling their dinner.

Barbecuing suits the casual outdoorsy sort of life we lead; it's part of our culture, bringing family groups or friends together in an informal setting where matching crockery and the correct way to hold a knife don't seem to matter. It's ingrained in our souls and I love it as much as anyone.

While the barbecue ethos hasn't changed since my youth, what we cook and what we cook it on *has*, and the stereotype of the male standing at the barbecue having a few beers with his mates while he incinerates a few sausages has been surpassed. Still, as a woman, I had to elbow my way in to get a go on the grill – men loving fire and all that – but once there, I've never looked back.

What I like best about barbecuing is the resinous perfume of rosemary as it suffuses warming oil with its sweet pungency, the smell of smoke and caramel as red peppers blister and char, the way chicken sizzles and slowly turns crusty and golden brown, the sound of bacon rashers as they spit and frizzle to golden, salty deliciousness, and the drama of steaks as they hiss and flare until the grill beats them into crisp and seared submission. Barbecuing puts you in touch with the food you are cooking, you can see it, you can smell it and you can hear it cooking. Then there are those sneaky titbits you get to nibble under the pretence of 'just checking to see how things are going', and the adulation you receive when you finally present your masterpiece. All these things add to the thrill of the grill. It's addictive. And all the while, the spitting and spluttering is not going over the kitchen floor and walls. There's a certain freedom in that, in letting Mother Nature wash it all away with a shower of rain, or burn it off with the heat of the sun.

I've written hundreds of recipes for barbecues over the years. Putting them in some sort of order seemed a logical thing to do: it would save me having to hunt through heaps of magazine articles (written before computers were part of our lives) for my favourite way with lamb or prawns or aubergine. The idea for a book was born. I wanted the book to be a collection of standout recipes – things that you'd really feel like cooking because they're so gobsmackingly good – and to have some basics, too, such as cooking a steak well, because it is easy to presume that everyone already knows these things.

This is it, then, **Sizzle**. Sensational recipes to see you through summer, autumn, winter and spring; recipes to cook outside in the sun, but many with indoor cooking instructions as well in case the weather turns on you; recipes for meat-lovers and vegetarians alike; recipes for you to cook for your lover, your mother or your kids; and recipes for your kids to cook for you. Family food, mid-week meals, feasts and sumptuous spreads are all here.

Sizzle is for all you barbecue grillers out there who are looking for a few tips to spruce up your act (check out Barbecue Know-how at the back of the book), or for an armful of gorgeous, finger-licking recipes that you can put your stamp on and call your own: recipes that will please the crowds, and please you with their ease of making, stylish looks and drop-dead deliciousness. And for those of you who are new to barbecuing, all the basics are covered. I heartily recommend grabbing the tongs and having a go.

beginnings

Little tastes, food to share, dishes to tease the appetite, the

beginnings of a meal are all these things. Once aromas waft from the

barbecue, stomachs rumble. It doesn't have to be difficult . . . but it does

have to be tasty.

above: bruschetta with roasted cherry tomatoes page 32
right: barbecued garlic bread page 22

Tessa's barbecued crab cakes with Cambodian dressing

SERVES 6 OR MORE (MAKES ABOUT 36 SMALL CAKES)

These are best served at the beach. With the salt air teasing your nostrils and wearing your oldest clothes, you can slurp and dribble to your heart's content. They are simply the best crab cakes ever.

DRESSING

10 cloves garlic, peeled, finely
   chopped then lightly crushed

3 medium–hot red chillies, deseeded
   and very finely chopped

juice of 2 or more lemons

¼ cup water

1 tsp fish sauce

1 tsp salt

3 tsp sugar

CRAB CAKES

250g fresh crab meat, picked over,
   or use canned crab meat

250g white fish fillets, rinsed and
   coarsely chopped

¼ cup of the thick part of a can of
   coconut cream (see Glossary)

¼ tsp salt

oil for barbecuing

TO SERVE

1–2 iceberg lettuces, torn apart,
   washed and dried

1–2 cups coriander sprigs

1–2 cups mint leaves

extra lemon wedges for serving

DRESSING

1 Mix together all dressing ingredients; taste and adjust for desired sourness, saltiness and pungency. Dressing will keep in the fridge in a covered glass bowl or jar for 3–4 days.

CRAB CAKES

1 In the bowl of a food processor, quickly pulse together crab meat, fish, coconut cream and salt 30–40 times or until amalgamated. Roll mixture into balls in the palms of your hands, making them about the size of walnuts in the shell. Put them on a plate (crab cakes can be prepared a few hours ahead to this point; keep them covered with plastic food wrap and refrigerated).

2 Cook the balls over a medium heat on an oiled barbecue hot plate, pressing them flat with a fish slice. Cook briefly until lightly browned on both sides.

3 Arrange crab cakes on a platter with lettuce, herbs and lemon wedges and serve dressing in a small bowl. Let everyone make their own crab rolls by enclosing a crab cake in a lettuce leaf, spooning plenty of dressing over and adding a garnish of herbs. Roll up and devour!

dribble to your heart's content...

roll up and devour!

Asparagus & mint prosciutto wraps

SERVES 4

These asparagus wraps are imbued with a hint of caramelly smokiness. The salt 'hit' from crisp prosciutto is wiped clean by lemon and mint, making them irresistible. You can make up the wraps a few hours before cooking as long as you keep them refrigerated, but bring them to room temperature before cooking. Accompany with lemon wedges or a spicy dipping sauce.

12 plump asparagus spears
grated zest of 1 lemon
2 Tbsp extra virgin olive oil
sea salt and freshly ground black pepper
100g thinly sliced prosciutto or equivalent amount of
shaved ham
48 mint leaves
lemon wedges to accompany or a spicy dipping sauce of
your choice

1   Snap off the woody ends from the asparagus spears or trim them with a knife. Wash asparagus under running water; soak if gritty.

2   In a large shallow dish mix together lemon zest and oil with a few pinches of salt and plenty of black pepper. Add spears and roll them around in the dish to coat.

3   Wrap each spear in a slice of prosciutto or ham, enclosing four mint leaves with each spear.

4   Cook asparagus wraps over a medium heat on an oiled barbecue hot plate, turning often, until they turn a rich golden brown (about 10 minutes). Serve hot.

Barbecued sweet corn

SERVES 6

Fresh corn really captures the essence of summer for me and when it's combined with a whiff of barbecue smoke, I'm done for. Cooked on the barbecue, the kernels steam and become tender, and the natural sugars caramelise, developing a gorgeously sweet and nutty flavour.

6 fresh sweet corn cobs
extra virgin olive oil, preferably a fruity-tasting one
sea salt
chilli powder
freshly ground black pepper
lime wedges
butter

natural string for tying corn

1   To cook the corn cobs in their husks, first remove the silks. Pull down the husks leaf by leaf to reveal the silks, then remove. Replace leaves carefully; tie with string to secure. Soak cobs in cold water for 30 minutes.

2   Cook cobs in hot coals for 15–30 minutes, turning often. Alternatively, cook cobs on a barbecue hot plate, splashing them with a little water from time to time, for about 30 minutes or until the kernels are browned.

3   Serve corn cobs drizzled with oil and dusted with sea salt, chilli powder and a little black pepper, accompanied with lime wedges or, more simply, with lashings of butter, sea salt and black pepper.

Aubergine & red pepper crostini

SERVES 6–8 AS A HEFTY SNACK OR 3–4 AS A LIGHT MEAL

This is just the ticket when you want more than a bowl of nuts, but it's also great served with a salad as a light meal.

1 medium aubergine (eggplant)
olive oil
salt
2 large red peppers (capsicums)
50g butter, softened
3 black olives, stoned and chopped
2 cloves garlic, peeled and crushed
**½ baguette (French bread) or 8 slices of a ciabatta loaf
    (slipper-shaped sourdough loaf)**
freshly ground black pepper
¼ cup tiny basil leaves (or chopped basil leaves)
1 Tbsp balsamic vinegar
1 Tbsp extra virgin olive oil

1   Slice aubergine into rounds and dunk slices in olive oil. Cook over high heat on a barbecue hot plate until very tender and a deep golden colour. Sprinkle with salt and transfer to a plate.

2   Cook peppers over medium heat on a barbecue grill rack, turning them with tongs until blackened on both sides. Transfer peppers to a plate and allow to cool. Peel off blackened skins, rinsing your hands as you do this, but don't put peppers under running water or you'll rinse away the flavour. Cut peppers in half. Remove cores and seeds, reserving juices, and cut flesh into strips. Alternatively, cook peppers in the hot coals of a barbecue or in the oven. To cook them in the oven, put peppers on a rack in the oven preheated to 180°C and cook for about 20 minutes or until blistered and charred. Transfer to a bowl, cover and when cool enough to handle, peel off blackened skins and discard cores and seeds. Chop peppers into strips and set aside with the juices. (The peppers can be roasted the day before required; cover and chill.)

3   In a small bowl mix together butter, olives and garlic. Slice bread thinly and lightly spread both sides with olive butter. Cook bread slices over a gentle heat on a barbecue hot plate until golden; if heat is too fierce, bread will quickly blacken. Alternatively, put bread slices on a baking sheet and bake in an oven preheated to 180°C for about 12 minutes or until crisp and golden.

4   To assemble crostini, cut eggplant slices in halves or quarters and arrange on top of toasted bread rounds. Mound sliced peppers on top. Mix pepper juices with a few pinches of salt, plenty of black pepper, basil leaves, balsamic vinegar and oil. Spoon this dressing over crostini and serve.

Courgette & corn fritters

MAKES ABOUT 24 LARGE FRITTERS OR 40 MINI ONES

These fritters are a real taste of summer. Team them up with tomato chutney or chilli sauce, and maybe a salad and a little crispy bacon on the side.

250g small courgettes (zucchini)
salt
3 fresh sweet corn cobs
3 spring onions, trimmed and chopped
2 Tbsp chopped parsley
1 Tbsp chopped marjoram
4 medium eggs, lightly beaten
freshly ground black pepper
2 Tbsp plain flour
olive oil for frying
spicy tomato chutney or sweet chilli sauce for
**   serving (optional)**

1   Grate courgettes coarsely and transfer to a colander. Sprinkle with salt and leave to drain for 30 minutes. Squeeze out the moisture, then wrap grated courgettes in absorbent kitchen paper and mop dry. Transfer to a bowl.

2   Remove husks and silks from corn cobs, then boil gently for about 12 minutes or until tender. Drain, then drape cobs with a piece of absorbent kitchen paper until cool enough to handle. Using a large sharp knife, cut the kernels off the cobs and add kernels to bowl of courgettes. (Vegetables can be prepared 1–2 hours ahead to this point; cover and refrigerate.)

3   Add spring onions, parsley, marjoram, eggs, ¾ teaspoon of salt and plenty of pepper. Blend in flour.

4   Drop tablespoonfuls of batter onto a hot well-oiled barbecue hot plate and cook until golden. Turn fritters over and cook other side. Drain fritters briefly on crumpled absorbent kitchen paper. Alternatively, heat ½ cup oil in a large frying pan over a medium heat. When oil is hot, but before it starts hazing, drop tablespoonfuls of mixture in the hot oil. Fry until golden, turn and cook on other side, then drain briefly on absorbent kitchen paper. Transfer to a serving plate and serve immediately.

Panzanella

SERVES 4–6

Traditionally, panzanella (Italian bread salad) was a home for leftover dried bread, which was soaked in water or dressings to bring it back to life. I think it is much nicer made with toasted bread – choose a good structured sourdough loaf, or a well-made baguette, not fluffy white stuff. The salad is at its best about 30 minutes after tossing the croûtons through because the hard edges of the croûtons soften a little and absorb some of the scrummy juices, but they haven't completely softened. This timing makes it a perfect dish for a barbecue – do the bread first, then barbecue the rest of the meal. Serve panzanella as a starter or as an accompanying salad.

½ small ciabatta loaf (slipper-shaped sourdough loaf) or ½ baguette (French bread)
olive oil or olive oil spray
2 small red onions, peeled and thinly sliced
½ telegraph cucumber (long, tender-skinned cucumber)
3 large tomatoes, cubed and drained briefly
½ cup black olives
½ cup basil leaves
1 clove garlic, peeled and crushed
1 Tbsp capers, drained
salt and freshly ground black pepper
4 Tbsp extra virgin olive oil
1 Tbsp red wine vinegar

1   Cut bread into 1.5cm cubes to generously fill 2 cups. Put bread cubes in a shallow dish and drizzle or spray lightly with oil. Cook for a few minutes on each side until golden on a barbecue hot plate. Transfer croûtons to a side plate.

2   Soak sliced onions in cold water for 15 minutes. Peel cucumber, cut in half lengthways, scoop out seeds, then cut into half circles. Transfer cucumber to a large bowl, add drained onions, cubed tomatoes, olives and croûtons. Tear the larger basil leaves into small pieces and scatter them over the top.

3   In a small bowl mix together garlic and capers with ½ teaspoon of salt, and pepper to taste. Add oil and vinegar and pour over salad. Toss well, then cover and chill for 30–45 minutes. Garnish with remaining basil leaves before serving.

the croûtons soften a little and absorb some of the

scrummy juices

Prawns with fennel seed butter

SERVES 6

These are finger-licking good– just as prawns should be! They are best cooked on flat-edged skewers because they'll flop around on thin metal ones. To serve for a main course, add bowls of steaming fragrant rice and a salad of slivered fresh fennel with loads of fresh mint, dressed with a lemony vinaigrette.

1kg green (raw) king prawns

100g butter, melted

finely grated zest of 1 lemon
and 1 lime

juice of 1 lemon

2 cloves garlic, peeled and crushed

½ tsp salt

½ tsp fennel seeds

¼ tsp ground cinnamon

½ tsp freshly ground coriander
seeds

2 tiny dried bird's eye chillies,
crushed

flat-edged skewers (if using
bamboo skewers, soak in
cold water for 30 minutes before
using)

1   If prawns are frozen, thaw them slowly in the fridge or quickly in a sealed plastic bag immersed in hot water. Twist off their heads, then peel off shells, leaving the small piece on the tail intact. Using a sharp knife, slit down the back of each prawn and gently extract the black or red vein. Rinse prawns, then pat dry with absorbent kitchen paper.

2   Put the butter in a bowl and add the remaining ingredients.

3   Oil skewers lightly, then thread 3–4 prawns onto a skewer by curling each prawn tightly and piercing twice with the skewer. Transfer to a large flat dish and spoon over the spicy butter. Prawns can be prepared a few hours ahead to this point; cover and refrigerate but bring to room temperature before cooking.

4   Cook prawns over a medium heat on an oiled barbecue hot plate for 1–2 minutes (they'll quickly change to a pinky-coral colour), basting once or twice with the spice butter. Turn prawns over and cook on other side for 1–2 minutes until just cooked through. Serve hot.

Mango & prawn salad with cellophane noodles

SERVES 4 AS A STARTER OR LIGHT SALAD

Balance this light and fresh salad with a nice, hot bite of chilli. Serve before a seafood barbecue or Asian-style barbecued fish.

20 green (raw) king prawns
70g cellophane noodles
1 slightly unripe mango
½ small telegraph cucumber (long, tender-skinned cucumber)
½ cup lightly packed coriander leaves
2 Tbsp crisp fried shallots (available from Asian food stores) to garnish
chopped hot red chilli to garnish

DRESSING
4 Tbsp lime juice
1½ tsp caster sugar
1 Tbsp finely chopped fresh shallot
1 hot red chilli, deseeded and finely chopped
1½ Tbsp fish sauce

1   If prawns are frozen, thaw them slowly in the fridge or quickly in a sealed plastic bag immersed in hot water. Twist off their heads, then peel off shells, leaving the small piece on the tail intact. Using a sharp knife, slit down the back of each prawn and gently extract the black or red vein. Rinse prawns, then pat dry with absorbent kitchen paper.

2   Cook prawns over a high heat on a lightly oiled barbecue hot plate for a few minutes on each side until they turn a uniform pinky-coral colour. Transfer to a plate lined with absorbent kitchen paper. Alternatively, the prawns can be lightly poached.

3   Put cellophane noodles in a bowl, pour on hot water to cover (use boiled water that has been allowed to cool for 10 minutes) and leave for 7 minutes or until just tender, but still a little resilient. Drain, rinse under running cold water, then drain again. Snip the noodles with scissors several times to make them shorter in length and more manageable to eat.

4   Peel mango, then cut off the mango cheeks (fleshy parts) and any other flesh. Slice finely. Peel cucumber, cut in half and scoop out seeds. Cut cucumber into thin slices and put in a bowl with the mango.

5   Mix together dressing ingredients and pour over mango and cucumber. Add cooked prawns, coriander leaves and noodles and carefully toss together. Serve immediately garnished with crisp shallots and chilli.

Barbecued haloumi with grape salad

SERVES 3–4 AS A STARTER OR LIGHT LUNCH DISH

Salty and textural, haloumi cheese actually squeaks when you eat it! Serve it up the minute it comes off the hot plate, while it is still hot and supple. The grape salad counters the saltiness, and along with the fresh flavours of mint and lemon thyme, turns this into a memorable dish.

250g haloumi cheese
butter
freshly ground black pepper
1 lemon, cut into wedges

SALAD
3 Tbsp extra virgin olive oil
1 Tbsp verjuice (or white wine)
2 tsp creamy Dijon mustard
½ tsp salt
freshly ground black pepper to taste
1 small buttercrunch lettuce, leaves
**   washed and dried**
½ cup mint leaves
1 tsp lemon thyme (or 1 tsp thyme
**   and a little grated lemon zest)**
1 cup red grapes, halved and
**   deseeded**

1 Cut cheese into 5mm slices and pat dry with absorbent kitchen paper.

2 Whisk oil, verjuice, mustard, salt and pepper in a bowl. Add lettuce, torn into bite-sized pieces, mint leaves (tear if large), thyme and grapes. Toss and dish immediately onto individual plates. Ensure everyone is ready to eat as soon as the cheese comes off the barbecue.

4 Cook cheese slices in sizzling butter over medium heat on a barbecue hot plate until lightly golden, then turn over carefully and cook on other side. Season cheese with a little black pepper and a squeeze of lemon juice, then dish onto the salads. Serve immediately.

serve it up the minute it comes off the hot plate, while it is still soft and supple

Barbecued garlic bread

SERVES 4

Crisp and buttery garlic bread cooked in the oven is delicious, but this no-fuss barbecue version using olive oil is even better!

1 baguette (French bread)
150ml extra virgin olive oil
2 cloves garlic, peeled and crushed
2 Tbsp roughly chopped rosemary sprigs
sea salt

small bamboo skewers, soaked in cold water for
   30 minutes

1   Slice bread into rounds, then in half again. Put oil, garlic and rosemary in a large bowl and add bread pieces. Toss everything together, making sure all the bread gets coated with oil.

2   Slide bread pieces onto bamboo skewers, four chunks to each skewer. Garlic bread can be prepared several hours ahead to this point; keep covered.

3   Cook bread over a gentle heat on a barbecue hot plate until golden; if heat is too fierce, the bread will blacken too quickly. Season with a few pinches of salt and serve hot or add to salads such as Panzanella (see page 16).

Fresh sweet corn fritters

MAKES ABOUT 30 LARGE FRITTERS

These are good enough to turn into a light meal with bacon, baked tomatoes or a tomato salad and a crusty loaf, or serve them as a starter, topped with a blob of hot salsa.

6 fresh sweet corn cobs
3 spring onions, chopped
2 Tbsp chopped parsley
2 Tbsp chopped basil
5 medium eggs, lightly beaten
¼ cup cream
1 tsp salt
freshly ground black pepper
3 Tbsp plain flour
olive oil for frying
salsa or hot sauce of your choice for serving

1   Remove husks and silks from corn cobs, then boil gently for about 12 minutes or until tender. Drain, then drape cobs with a large piece of absorbent kitchen paper until cool enough to handle. Using a large sharp knife, cut the kernels off the cobs.

2   Put corn kernels in a bowl and add spring onions, parsley, basil, eggs, cream, salt and pepper to taste. Mix well, then blend in the flour.

3   Drop tablespoonfuls of the mixture onto a hot well-oiled barbecue hot plate. Cook fritters until golden on both sides. Drain fritters briefly on some crumpled absorbent kitchen paper. Transfer to a serving plate and serve immediately with a biting salsa or sweet Thai chilli sauce.

Scampi on the barbie

SERVES 4

Scampi, similar to shrimp, are easy enough to prepare and they're quick to cook, too; just watch out for the sharp bits. Although there is not much of it, the flesh is tender and sweet.

600g scampi
3 Tbsp lemon juice
3 Tbsp olive oil
few pinches of sea salt
freshly ground black pepper to taste
¼ tsp paprika
1 clove garlic, peeled and finely chopped
3 Tbsp snipped chives
1 Tbsp lemon thyme

1   Use scissors to snip both sides of the soft undershell of each scampi, then remove and discard. Rinse and shake dry.

2   In a shallow dish mix together remaining ingredients and add scampi. Spoon marinade over scampi and leave to marinate for 20 minutes at room temperature.

3   Put scampi, shell-side down, over a medium-hot barbecue grill rack or on the hot plate for 3–4 minutes. Spoon over some of the marinade, then turn and cook the underside of each for 1 minute more or until just cooked through. Serve hot, with finger bowls on the side.

sea air...

a sprinkle of paprika

and a few flecks of green

on coral-pink shells...

Pots of gold

SERVES 4–6

These are like single-serve cheese fondues, all gorgeous and gooey.

6 medium vine-ripened
   tomatoes, diced and briefly
   drained
small handful of fresh basil leaves,
   chopped
sea salt and freshly ground black
   pepper
lemon juice
extra virgin olive oil
4 cups salad leaves (rocket,
   watercress, red lettuce, sorrel,
   etc), washed and dried
white wine vinegar
1 baguette (French bread), pide
   (flat Turkish bread) or ciabatta
   loaf (slipper-shaped sourdough
   loaf)
2 large cloves garlic, peeled

small camembert or brie cheeses
   (1 per person), at room
   temperature

1 Make a simple tomato salad with diced tomatoes, chopped basil and a little salt, black pepper, a few squirts of lemon juice and a good dousing of olive oil.

2 Dress salad leaves with a splash of vinegar, salt, black pepper and a little olive oil.

3 Slice the baguette, pide or ciabatta and toast pieces over a barbecue grill rack. As they are done rub them, one at a time, with a whole garlic clove. Season with a little sea salt, then stack them one on top of the other.

4 When salads and bread are both ready, cook cheeses. Place them on an oiled grill rack over a medium heat. Cook for about 5 minutes or until lightly coloured, then turn them over carefully and cook on other side for a few minutes until cheeses feel soft and runny when gently squeezed around the waist. Carefully transfer cheeses to individual serving plates. To eat, make a shallow cut on top of cheese and partially peel back skin. Dunk in bread and go for it! Serve the salads on the side.

lovers of runny, gooey cheese

will go nuts over these

Bruschetta with chick pea pâté & sugared tomatoes

SERVES 6

This quick chick pea pâté can be made up to a day ahead.

1 x 310g can chick peas, drained,
   rinsed and drained again
salt and freshly ground black pepper
2 Tbsp lemon juice
1 clove garlic, peeled and crushed
extra virgin olive oil
1 Tbsp finely chopped parsley
1 Tbsp finely chopped mint, plus
   whole leaves for garnishing
6 medium vine-ripened tomatoes
caster sugar
1 tsp thyme leaves
1 small sourdough loaf, or baguette
   (French bread), or ciabatta
   (slipper-shaped sourdough loaf),
   sliced
1 large clove garlic, peeled and
   halved

1   Put the chick peas in the bowl of a food processor with ¼ teaspoon of salt, a good grind of black pepper, lemon juice, crushed garlic, and 1 tablespoon of extra virgin olive oil. Add 1 tablespoon of water and process until smooth, adding a little extra water if the mixture is too thick. Transfer pâté to a bowl and blend in parsley and mint. Cover and chill until required, but bring to room temperature before serving.

2   Rub the tomatoes with oil, cut in half and sprinkle the cut sides with salt and a dusting of caster sugar. Sprinkle over the thyme leaves. Cook tomatoes on a heated oiled barbecue hot plate, cut-side down, until lightly browned. Turn tomatoes over and cook briefly, then transfer to a plate.

3   Gently toast the slices of bread over a barbecue grill rack. Transfer to a board, rub each slice with the cut garlic, drizzle over a little extra virgin olive oil and sprinkle with salt. Spoon on the chick pea pâté and top with roasted tomatoes and mint leaves. Serve immediately. Alternatively, serve the bruschetta, pâté and tomatoes separately and let everyone assemble their own.

Sizzled scallops with coriander & chives

SERVES 4 AS A STARTER

Some people enjoy the orange-coloured coral (roe) attached to the scallop, but if that's not your custom, slice it off by all means. The scallops can be coated in the butter mixture a few hours before cooking (just keep them covered and refrigerated), then they're ready to fling on the barbecue when it suits you.

70g butter
2 small cloves garlic, peeled and
    crushed
1 Tbsp chopped coriander
1 Tbsp snipped chives
salt and freshly ground black pepper
400g scallops, rinsed and patted dry
2 medium vine-ripened tomatoes,
    skinned
½ tsp freshly ground coriander
    seeds
75ml extra virgin olive oil
1 Tbsp lemon juice
3 cups loosely packed lamb's lettuce
    (also known as corn salad or
    mâche) or use mixed baby salad
    greens
2 plain English muffins, split, or
    8 slices from a baguette (French
    bread)

1   In a small bowl mix together half the butter with the garlic and set aside.

2   In another bowl mix remaining butter with the herbs. Add a pinch of salt and a grind of black pepper, then gently melt butter; don't allow it to get too hot or it will start to cook the scallops. Add scallops and turn in bowl to coat. Set aside, refrigerated, for 1–2 hours.

3   Halve tomatoes, discard cores and flick out seeds. Dice flesh and set aside.

4   Cook scallops over a high heat on a barbecue hot plate for a few minutes on each side, sprinkling with ground coriander seeds as they cook, until browned and just cooked through.

5   Mix together oil and lemon juice with ½ teaspoon of salt and some black pepper. Wash lamb's lettuce, discarding any small roots, then dry in a salad spinner or with a clean tea towel. Put greens in a bowl, pour on dressing and toss lightly. Add diced tomatoes and toss again lightly. Toast muffins or baguette slices, spread with the garlic butter and divide between four plates. Top with a handful of salad, then several scallops. Serve immediately.

Goat's cheese bruschetta with grilled artichokes

SERVES 6

Slather garlicky bruschetta with a mild, lemony goat's cheese and top it with ready-made char-grilled artichokes for a quick and stylish snack.

**1 ciabatta loaf (slipper-shaped
   sourdough loaf)**
2 large cloves garlic, split
extra virgin olive oil
sea salt
100g mild, lemony goat's cheese
**280g jar char-grilled artichokes in oil, drained
   and chopped**
handful of fresh basil leaves

1   Slice ciabatta and toast on a barbecue grill rack until lightly charred on both sides. Rub each slice with cut garlic, transfer bread to a plate, drizzle with a little oil and sprinkle with a little salt.

2   Spread with goat's cheese and top with artichokes. Garnish with basil leaves and serve immediately.

Barbecued asparagus with buffalo mozzarella

SERVES 4

This is a superb combination. Buffalo mozzarella is softer in texture and milder in flavour than cow's milk mozzarella.

500g plump asparagus, trimmed
extra virgin olive oil
salt and freshly ground black pepper
250g ball buffalo mozzarella, drained
2 juicy oranges, peeled and sliced
8 smallish vine-ripened tomatoes, thickly sliced
handful of small basil leaves
good crusty bread for serving

1   Put asparagus in a flat dish, drizzle with oil and season with salt and pepper. Toss gently to coat spears with oil.

2   Cook asparagus over a hot barbecue grill rack for a few minutes on each side until lightly charred, turning with tongs; the asparagus should remain crunchy.

3   Pat mozzarella dry with absorbent kitchen paper, then slice it thinly.

4   Arrange sliced oranges and tomatoes on a serving platter or on individual plates. Top with mozzarella, basil and finally the asparagus. Grind over a little more pepper and drizzle with olive oil. Serve immediately with bread.

Seared scallops with chilli pepper dressing

SERVES 6

Cutting a criss-cross pattern on the scallops makes them open much like blooming flowers, letting them absorb more dressing as they cook, but this step is optional.

**rind of 1 lemon taken off in thick
strips**
1 Tbsp lemon juice
4 Tbsp extra virgin olive oil
salt and freshly ground black pepper
**½ large red pepper (capsicum),
deseeded and finely diced**
500g scallops, rinsed and patted dry
**2 tiny dried bird's eye chillies,
crushed**
handful of small basil leaves

1   Set aside rind before halving and squeezing lemon. Put juice in a bowl with 2 tablespoons of oil, ¼ teaspoon of salt and pepper to taste.

2   Put red pepper in a frying pan or saucepan with 1 tablespoon of oil and cook gently until tender. Cool, then add to dressing.

3   Score one side of each scallop (not the coral; remove the coral if you wish) in a criss-cross pattern using the point of a sharp knife. Put scallops in a bowl and drizzle over 1 tablespoon of oil. Add chillies and lemon rind. Gently toss scallops until they are coated with oil.

4   Cook scallops, scored-side down to begin with, over a medium heat on a barbecue hot plate for a few minutes on each side until nearly cooked through. Cook the lemon rind too, until golden. Transfer scallops to a serving dish as they are done, pour over the dressing and garnish with basil leaves and cooked lemon rind. Serve immediately.

sizzling lemon zest...

sea-fresh scallops

Bruschetta with roasted cherry tomatoes

SERVES 4

Bruschetta with tomatoes is a classic antipasto. Use the sweetest tomatoes you can find – this will contrast with the bitter edge they develop as they singe in the fire.

4 small branches cherry tomatoes or
    very small vine-ripened tomatoes
1 ciabatta loaf (slipper-shaped
    sourdough loaf)
2 plump cloves garlic, peeled
sea salt and freshly ground black
    pepper
extra virgin olive oil for drizzling

1   Slice ciabatta in half lengthways, then slice again through the middle of each half to yield four long quarters.

2   To cook tomatoes in hot coals, first soak whole bunches of unskinned tomatoes still on the branch in cold water for 10 minutes. Put tomatoes on red-hot coals, greenery down. They will start to blister after a few minutes. Turn carefully using long tongs and cook the other side for a few minutes. Fan the coals to create a little smoke if necessary. Put tomatoes on a plate and allow to cool. Remove skins, taking care not to rub any ash onto the tomato flesh.

3   Alternatively, put tomatoes in a shallow ovenproof dish (e.g. Swiss roll tin) lined with baking paper to make cleaning easier and drizzle with oil. Roast the tomatoes in an oven preheated to 250°C for 5–7 minutes or until tomatoes are just starting to collapse and char.

4   Toast bread on the barbecue grill rack until deeply golden (don't let it burn) and immediately rub each piece on the crumb side (not the crust side) with a cut clove of garlic. Put a branch of roasted tomatoes on each piece of bruschetta, season with a little salt and pepper and drizzle generously with oil. Serve immediately.

main events

Crank up the barbecue and let it be the scene-stealer with sizzling steaks and cutlets and spicy satay – or, equally appealing, with polenta and creamy mushrooms, spicy couscous, aubergine toasties or melting mozzarella kebabs.

above: spicy lamb on sticks with yoghurt sauce page 44
right: lamb cutlets with mustard & thyme page 54

Barbecued poussins

SERVES 6 OR MORE

This is an easy way to prepare young chickens – and splitting them in half ensures even cooking. If serving them as part of a big meal, half a poussin per person is generally sufficient, but if serving them with just a salad and bread, for instance, three-quarters to a whole poussin should be allowed.

**6 poussins (very young chickens),
  about 350g each**
8 cloves garlic, peeled and crushed
**1 loosely packed cup finely chopped
  coriander (or a blend, e.g. parsley,
  rosemary and marjoram)**
1 Tbsp freshly ground black pepper
2 tsp salt
½ cup lemon juice
4 Tbsp melted butter

1 Start preparation of poussins the day before cooking them. Using scissors, cut off necks if still attached, and pull off any visible fat. Slice each poussin down the length of the backbone, then snip through bone using poultry shears (or strong scissors). Turn poussins over and press flat by dislocating ball and socket joints of legs and wings (where they join the carcass).

2 In a small bowl mix remaining ingredients except the butter and paint over poussins with a soft brush. Pile poussins in a dish, one on top of the other, cover with plastic food wrap and refrigerate until the next day.

3 Take poussins out of fridge, turn over and spoon on juices. Return them to fridge, but bring to room temperature 1 hour before cooking. Reserve marinade for basting.

4 To barbecue poussins, allow 45–60 minutes cooking time over a medium heat. Brush skin side of poussins with the melted butter and cook this side first on the barbecue hot plate, then flip over and cook underside. Baste and turn poussins until cooked all the way through. Lower heat if poussins are cooking too quickly. If marinade runs out, use a little more melted butter. Poussins should be crisp and golden with tender, juicy flesh. Serve garnished with a bouquet of fresh herbs.

5 Alternatively, poussins can be partially barbecued until lightly coloured (which will give a mild barbecue taste), then placed in roasting tins and finished off in an oven preheated to 180°C. This is ideal if serving the poussins as part of a barbecue feast, as it frees the barbecue for other cooking.

Polenta toasties with garlicky mushroom sauce

SERVES 6

Here's a recipe to wow your vegetarian friends. If serving as a main course, accompany the toasties with a selection of salads. Alternatively, serve as a starter. Fast-cooking polenta (instant polenta), which cooks in about 5 minutes, can be used in this recipe.

1.25l water
salt
250g coarse polenta

MUSHROOM SAUCE
1 Tbsp butter
300g button mushrooms, thickly
   sliced
2 large cloves garlic, peeled and
   crushed
½ cup cream
salt and freshly ground black pepper
1 Tbsp each chopped parsley
   and mint
1 Tbsp snipped chives

1 Make the polenta first (can be prepared 1–2 days before finishing off this recipe; cover well and refrigerate).

2 Bring water to the boil in a large saucepan. Put polenta in a bowl. Add 1 teaspoon of salt to water then, keeping water at boiling point, sprinkle in polenta by taking a fistful and letting it run through your fingers into the water. Stir continuously with a wooden spoon as you do so. If polenta is added faster than this, it will form lumps that will not break down during cooking. If any polenta remains on the surface of the water, stir it in before sprinkling on more polenta, otherwise it, too, will form lumps (if lumps form, fish them out with a spoon).

3 Turn heat to low and cook, stirring continually, for 20 minutes. Heat should be low enough so that polenta is not 'plopping' or splattering, but rather just about to plop or splatter. Cook until mixture is so thick that the wooden spoon will stand upright in centre of pan; a fail-proof sign that it is cooked. If using 'instant' polenta, cook as indicated on the packet.

4 Tip polenta onto a wet tray and spread it about 1–1.5cm thick. Smooth out surface and allow to cool. Cut cooled polenta into squares and cook over medium heat on a clean, lightly oiled barbecue hot plate until browned. Dish onto heated serving plates and top with hot Mushroom Sauce.

MUSHROOM SAUCE
1 Heat a frying pan over a medium heat and drop in the butter. Once it is sizzling, add mushrooms. Cook, tossing continuously, until lightly browned and tender. Add garlic and cook for 1–2 minutes until nutty-smelling. Tip in cream, add ¼ teaspoon of salt, and black pepper to taste, and cook until thickish and creamy. Mix in herbs and spoon immediately over squares of barbecued polenta.

Seared lamb with cumin rub

SERVES 6–8

Lamb shortloins are thin strips of prime meat. All they need is a little seasoning and a quick sear on the hot plate to arrive at tender succulence. Served with these salads, they make an outstanding dish.

BEETROOT SALAD
800g small beetroot
1 Tbsp lemon juice
finely grated zest of 1 lemon
2 Tbsp extra virgin olive oil
salt and freshly ground black pepper
½ cup chopped fresh walnuts

CUCUMBER AND YOGHURT SALAD
1 telegraph cucumber (long, tender-skinned cucumber), peeled
salt
300ml thick Greek yoghurt
2 cloves garlic, peeled and crushed
3 Tbsp chopped mint

LAMB
1 Tbsp ground toasted cumin seeds
1 Tbsp sea salt
1 tsp freshly ground black pepper
1 Tbsp soft butter
4 lamb shortloins (about 900g)

2–3 handfuls of rocket
extra virgin olive oil
salt and freshly ground black pepper
1 cup slow-roasted or semi-dried tomatoes (homemade or buy ready-made to save time!)
baps (soft bread buns) or pita pockets

BEETROOT SALAD

1 Wash beetroot carefully, put them in a saucepan and cover with cold water. Bring to the boil, lower heat, partially cover with a lid and cook gently until tender or until the skin will wrinkle easily (about 45 minutes). Drain.

2 When beetroot are cool, slip off skins and cut into large cubes. Mix lemon juice, zest and oil together, adding ½ teaspoon of salt and a little black pepper, and toss cubed beetroot. Just before serving, add walnuts.

CUCUMBER AND YOGHURT SALAD

1 Halve cucumber lengthways and scoop out seeds. Slice each half into thinnish half-moons. Transfer to a colander, salt lightly and leave to drain for 15 minutes. Pat dry with absorbent kitchen paper.

2 In a bowl mix together yoghurt, garlic and mint. Add cucumber. Although mixture may seem quite stiff, it will thin a little as it stands. Chill for 1 hour before serving.

LAMB

1 Mix cumin, salt, pepper and butter. Smear over the lamb and leave meat at room temperature for 30 minutes, covered.

2 Cook lamb over a gentle heat on a barbecue hot plate for about 5 minutes on each side. Allow it to brown nicely but it should remain medium–rare inside; it will continue to cook a little as it stands before slicing. Rest lamb for 5–7 minutes before slicing thinly. Season with more salt and let juices run a little before transferring slices to the platter of rocket.

3 Dress rocket with a little extra virgin olive oil, salt and pepper, and strew it over a serving plate. Arrange lamb on top along with slow-roasted tomatoes. Use fresh baps or pita pockets, or toast them if preferred. Encourage everyone to build their own bap with rocket, tomatoes, sliced lamb, Cucumber and Yoghurt Salad, and Beetroot Salad.

Polpettine

SERVES 4–6 (MAKES 16 SKEWERS)

These Italian 'meatballs on skewers' are deliciously flavoured with garlic, marjoram and mortadella, a large, lightly spiced sausage. The meatballs are interspersed with crusts of toasted bread and melting globs of gruyère cheese. Cor! Balance them with a salad of vine-ripened tomatoes dressed with extra virgin olive oil, a splash of balsamic vinegar and masses of torn fresh basil leaves.

600g mixed veal and pork mince (or use 100% pork mince)

1 large egg, lightly beaten

2 cloves garlic, peeled and crushed

salt and freshly ground black pepper to taste

a little freshly grated nutmeg

1 Tbsp finely chopped marjoram

½ cup (50g) freshly grated parmesan cheese

½ cup (30g) fresh breadcrumbs

75g mortadella sausage or ham, finely chopped

½ baguette (French loaf), cut into 32 cubes

200g gruyère cheese, cut into 16 cubes

OIL GLAZE

2 Tbsp olive oil

1 clove garlic, smashed with a mallet

freshly ground black pepper to taste

1 large sprig marjoram

16 bamboo skewers, soaked in cold water for 30 minutes

1 Put minced meat in a bowl, break it apart with a large fork and beat in egg, garlic, ½ teaspoon of salt, plenty of pepper, nutmeg, marjoram, parmesan cheese, breadcrumbs and mortadella. Blend thoroughly, then with wet hands shape into 32 ovals, putting them on a tray as they are prepared. Cover with plastic food wrap and chill for 2 hours (or overnight) to firm.

2 Make 16 skewers each with the following ingredients: 1 cube of bread, 1 meatball, 1 cube of gruyère cheese, a second meatball and another cube of bread. When all are prepared, cover and refrigerate until cooking time (skewers can be prepared a few hours ahead to this point).

3 In a small bowl mix ingredients for glaze. Gently brush skewers with glaze. Cook over a medium heat on an oiled barbecue hot plate. Don't be alarmed when cheese melts and oozes – scrape it back into shape as you turn skewers; it will turn crisp and golden and is part of the charm of these skewers. Cook until meat is browned and cooked through; you will need to test one (lucky cook!). Just be aware that both mortadella and ham give the meat an impression of not being cooked because they turn very pink when cooked. Serve hot.

Char-grilled lamb rumps with balsamic tomatoes

SERVES 4

These lamb rumps are excellent served with couscous, or a potato or kumara (sweet potato) mash.

150g Roma (oval-shaped) or fleshy tomatoes (don't use watery ones)
4 small lamb rumps, weighing about 150g each, trimmed
olive oil
salt and freshly ground black pepper
16 cherry tomatoes, washed and dried
4 Tbsp extra virgin olive oil
1 tsp ground coriander
splash of balsamic vinegar
2 Tbsp finely chopped mint
1 tsp chopped fresh rosemary

1 Skin tomatoes. Cut them in half, flick seeds into a sieve set over a bowl and leave seeds to drain. Dice tomato flesh.

2 Rub lamb rumps with olive oil and plenty of pepper. Cook rumps on a very hot barbecue grill rack to start, but lower heat after a few minutes and cook rumps gently until done to your liking (outside should be well seared; when meat is bouncy or springy to touch it is rare; when it still moves under pressure, but has lost bounce, it is medium; when it feels firm and offers no resistance to pressure, it is well done. My preference is between medium rare and medium, i.e. cooked for about 15–20 minutes).

3 Transfer lamb to a board and sprinkle both sides very generously with salt. Rest meat for 2–3 minutes to allow juices to be absorbed while preparing tomatoes.

4 Put 1 teaspoon of olive oil in a small frying pan and set it over a medium–high heat. When hot, tip in cherry tomatoes. Toss tomatoes in pan and cook for 20 seconds, until glazed. Turn tomatoes onto a plate and wipe out pan.

5 Warm the extra virgin olive oil in frying pan. Add ground coriander, then diced tomato and strained juice, a good splash of balsamic vinegar, ¼ teaspoon of salt and herbs. Warm jus through, then remove from heat.

6 Slice meat thinly across the grain and let it rest on a board for 1 minute, then transfer to heated serving plates. Spoon tomato jus over lamb and garnish with cherry tomatoes. Serve immediately.

Spicy lamb on sticks with yoghurt sauce

SERVES 3–4 (MAKES ABOUT 12 MEATBALLS)

A different way to present meatballs, in this case the minced lamb is flavoured with garlic, onion, coriander and garam masala. Chick pea flour is added to enrich and give body. The mixture is shaped into ovals about 5cm long, which are skewered, and cooked on a barbecue hot plate, then finished off over a flaming barbecue grill rack to impart a smoky flavour. Alternatively, cook these skewers on an oiled baking sheet under a preheated oven grill.

650g prime minced lamb (or beef)
1 medium onion, peeled and finely chopped
1 clove garlic, peeled and crushed
1 tsp finely grated fresh ginger
1½ tsp salt
1 tsp garam masala
2 Tbsp finely chopped coriander
1 egg
¼ cup water
2 Tbsp besan (chick pea flour)
fluffy steamed rice for serving (optional)

YOGHURT SAUCE
1 cup plain unsweetened yoghurt
pinch of salt
2 Tbsp chopped mint
1 hot green chilli, deseeded and finely chopped

1 Put minced meat in a large bowl and add onion, garlic, ginger, salt, garam masala and coriander. Beat egg and water together, add to minced meat mixture, then sprinkle on chick pea flour. Knead mixture together thoroughly with your hands.

2 Shape meat into small 'sausage' shapes, transferring them to a plate as they are prepared. Cover and chill meatballs for 1–2 hours before cooking them.

3 In a bowl mix ingredients for Yoghurt Sauce. Cover and set aside.

4 Put two meatballs on each skewer. The best skewers are the flatter kind; the meat flops around on smooth, round metal skewers (but if preferred you can forgo skewers and cook meatballs individually). Carefully transfer skewers to a lightly oiled barbecue hot plate and cook over a medium–high heat until cooked through (you'll need to cut one open to check). Finish cooking them over a hot barbecue grill rack. Serve hot with Yoghurt Sauce and plenty of fluffy steamed rice.

Lebanese meatballs

SERVES 4 (MAKES 20–24 MEATBALLS)

Choose a low-fat lamb mince for these meatballs and serve them piping hot off the grill.

750g prime minced lamb
1 small onion, peeled and finely chopped
1 clove garlic, peeled and crushed
1 egg, beaten
¼ tsp allspice
½ tsp ground cinnamon
1 tsp ground cumin
salt and freshly ground black pepper
2 Tbsp chopped mint
3 Tbsp chopped parsley
olive oil
accompanying salad (optional): chopped tomatoes,
   slivered red onions, sliced green pepper (capsicum),
   cos lettuce, black olives, lemon wedges and salt and
   pepper

1   Put minced lamb in a large bowl and add onion, garlic and beaten egg. Mix spices together with 1 teaspoon of salt and plenty of pepper and add to lamb with mint and parsley. Mix well.

2   Roll meat into oval shapes the size of an egg and thread onto heavyweight flat-edged metal skewers. Rub meatballs with oil, then cook over a medium heat on an oiled barbecue hot plate, or on a hot grill rack, until browned and just cooked through.

3   If liked, make a quick salad with tomatoes, red onion, green pepper and cos lettuce. Garnish salad with black olives, squeeze on some lemon juice and season with a little salt and pepper. Arrange meatballs on top and serve with more lemon wedges.

Chicken fillets with thyme

SERVES 4

Chicken fillets are thin and cook quickly, so keep an eye on them to ensure you end up with tender juicy morsels, not dried-out nuggets. Serve them on top of a mixed salad arranged on a platter. Include small new cooked potatoes, rocket, salad leaves, cherry tomatoes, olives, cucumber (or whatever combination you fancy), or stuff into baps or pita pockets with salad and a spicy chutney.

3 cloves garlic, peeled and cut into slivers
finely grated zest of 1 lemon
1 Tbsp freshly ground coriander seeds
1 Tbsp thyme leaves
2 Tbsp olive oil
freshly ground black pepper
700g chicken fillets (tenderloins)
sea salt

1   In a shallow dish mix garlic, lemon zest, ground coriander, thyme leaves, oil and plenty of black pepper. Add chicken fillets and turn to coat with marinade. Cover and chill for at least 1 hour, but up to 8 hours.

2   Remove chicken fillets from fridge 10 minutes before cooking them. Cook in batches over a medium heat on a barbecue hot plate for a few minutes on each side until golden but just cooked through. Sprinkle with salt. Cook garlic slices from marinade separately – so they don't burn – and remove them to a plate when they are pale golden in colour.

3   Dish chicken fillets onto a heated serving plate and spoon over garlic slivers. Serve immediately.

Mushroom burgers

SERVES 4 (MAKES 4 BURGERS)

These are unbelievably tender patties, with a rich meaty flavour. French fries and a crisp and crunchy salad make good accompaniments. If liked, put a little of the salad inside the bun with the patty.

100g brown button or field mushrooms, wiped clean
  and halved
salt and freshly ground black pepper
1 medium onion, peeled and roughly chopped
2 Tbsp soy sauce
500g minced topside beef or prime minced beef
1 clove garlic, peeled and crushed
4 Tbsp butter, softened
olive oil
4 hamburger buns, sesame seed buns or baps (soft
  bread buns)
1–2 very fresh mushrooms, wiped and sliced plus
  snipped chives to garnish (optional)

1   Put mushrooms in the bowl of a food processor or in a liquidiser and blend until finely chopped. Add ¼ teaspoon each of salt and pepper, then onion and soy sauce. Blend until liquefied. Put beef in a large bowl, add mushroom mixture and beat until thoroughly mixed. Cover and chill until required.

2   When ready to cook, mix crushed garlic and butter on a plate and set aside. Shape the meat into four patties. Cook patties over a medium heat on a well-oiled barbecue hot plate for 4–5 minutes on each side.

3   Meanwhile, toast buns and spread with the garlic butter. Place cooked patties on bun bases and garnish with 1–2 slices of fresh mushroom and a few snipped chives if liked. Put bun tops in place and serve immediately.

...baby buttons,

fresh and crisp and a

sprinkle of snipped

chives

Chicken skewers on watermelon & feta salad

SERVES 6 (MAKES APPROXIMATELY 24 SKEWERS)

Fresh and juicy, with a salty lick of feta, this dish is perfect for lunch on a hot summer's day or for a shared platter with friends on a balmy evening.

CHICKEN SKEWERS

2 yellow peppers (capsicums)

245g jar pimiento-stuffed green olives (or Queen olives, which are even better), drained

4 Tbsp olive oil

1 lemon

1 Tbsp honey

2 Tbsp finely chopped mint, plus extra sprigs for garnishing

salt and freshly ground black pepper

750g skinned and boned chicken breasts, cut into small pieces

SALAD

¼ cup pumpkin seeds

sea salt and freshly ground black pepper

2 cos lettuces (or 2 x 170g bags of cos leaves), broken into leaves, washed and dried

½ small watermelon, rind removed and cut into small chunks

250g feta cheese (choose a firmish kind), patted dry and crumbled into chunks

3 Tbsp lemon-infused extra virgin olive oil (or use extra virgin olive oil with the zest of 1 lemon)

1 Tbsp white wine vinegar

short bamboo skewers, soaked in cold water for 30 minutes

1 Core and deseed peppers and cut them into smallish chunks. Put in a bowl with olives and mix in 1 tablespoon of olive oil. Set aside for 15 minutes.

2 Peel off lemon rind in long thin strips and juice the lemon. Put rind in a bowl with strained lemon juice and honey, the rest of the oil, mint, ¼ teaspoon of salt and pepper. Mix well, then add chicken pieces, stirring well to coat. Thread chicken onto bamboo skewers alternating with chunks of yellow pepper and olives.

3 Cook over a medium heat on a barbecue hot plate until chicken is lightly browned and cooked through; do not have the heat too high or the outside of chicken will brown before the inside cooks properly. Drizzle with marinade during cooking, but take care that lemon rind does not burn. To avoid this happening, scrape pieces of lemon rind onto hot plate and cook separately until golden, then put on top of the skewers once they are cooked (they have a delicious intense lemony flavour).

4 Have ready a salad made with remaining ingredients. Cook pumpkin seeds first in a lightly oiled saucepan over a medium heat until they cease popping, shaking pan occasionally (pan must be covered either with a splatter screen or lid, because seeds pop everywhere and they're hot!). Tip seeds onto a plate and sprinkle generously with sea salt.

5 Arrange cos leaves on a large platter. Lay watermelon slices on leaves, crumble feta over, then scatter over pumpkin seeds. Mix lemon-infused olive oil and white wine vinegar with ¼ teaspoon of sea salt and some black pepper. Pour this over the salad. Put the hot chicken kebabs on top and garnish with mint sprigs. Serve immediately.

Aubergine toasties

SERVES 6

When aubergine is cooked well on the barbecue, by that I mean cooked until it is tender, golden, slightly charred and smelling a little smoky, woody and caramelised, it is food for the gods. While hot, sandwich the slices with fresh milky mozzarella cheese and nestle these bundles in seasoned bread, then cook until golden on the barbecue. Forget your manners, just bite through the melting threads of cheese and devour.

2 medium aubergines (eggplants), sliced

olive oil

150g fresh bocconcini mozzarella balls in whey, drained, patted dry and sliced not too thickly

soft butter

1 loaf grainy bread, sliced toast thickness

4 medium vine-ripened tomatoes

130g rocket leaves

1 cup small basil leaves

extra virgin olive oil

½ juicy lemon

sea salt and freshly ground black pepper

1 clove garlic, peeled and crushed and Dijon mustard (optional)

chilli jam or fruity chutney

1 Dunk aubergine slices in olive oil and cook on a barbecue hot plate until well browned (this is important – if they aren't cooked through they will taste astringent). Transfer them to a large plate as they are done, sandwiching two slices of eggplant together with two slices of mozzarella cheese in the middle.

2 Meanwhile, butter 12 slices of bread on one side only. When all aubergine is cooked, scrape barbecue plate as clean as possible and lower heat. Slice tomatoes and dress rocket leaves and basil with a little extra virgin olive oil, a few squirts of lemon juice, some sea salt and black pepper. Add a little crushed garlic and a dab of Dijon mustard if you like.

3 Put half the bread, buttered side down, on a board and spread with chilli jam or chutney. Put the aubergine and mozzarella bundles on the bread, season with salt and pepper and top with balance of bread, buttered side up.

4 Cook toasties over a medium heat on a barbecue hot plate until bread is golden, then flip over and cook other side. Using a metal spatula or similar, press down on toasties once or twice while cooking. Transfer to a chopping board. They're delicious as they are, but a few slices of tomato tucked into the sandwiches along with some of the dressed rocket and basil leaves makes a tasty addition. Alternatively, serve tomatoes and leaves separately. Serve hot or hottish, cut into halves or triangles. There may well be extra aubergine bundles – in which case, just butter some more bread!

...smelling a little smoky, woody and caramelised,

it is food for the gods

Barbecued lamb with spiced couscous

SERVES 6

Choose your preferred cut of lamb for this dish – it works well with all tender cuts. I have used lamb eye fillets in the photograph.

1 onion, peeled and finely chopped
olive oil
1 clove garlic, peeled and crushed
1 tsp each ground or crushed
   coriander seeds and fennel seeds
¼ tsp chilli powder
salt
200g 'instant' (quick-cooking)
couscous
300ml stock, heated (heat just before
using so it doesn't evaporate)
1 Tbsp chopped mint, plus extra for
   garnishing
1 Tbsp red wine vinegar
lamb (see note below)
1 Tbsp crushed coriander seeds
freshly ground black pepper
12 halves (about 60g) semi-dried
   tomatoes, chopped
1 char-grilled yellow pepper
   (capsicum), deseeded and chopped
   (see Couscous with chick peas &
   nuts, page 102)
½ cup black olives, drained
6 medium vine-ripened tomatoes,
   chopped

DRESSING
3 Tbsp extra virgin olive oil
1 Tbsp white wine vinegar
1 clove garlic, peeled and crushed
¼ tsp salt and pepper to taste
1 Tbsp chopped Italian parsley

1   Put onion in a medium-sized saucepan with 2 tablespoons of olive oil and cover with a lid. Cook gently until it is softened, but not coloured. Add garlic and crushed seeds, chilli powder and ½ teaspoon salt. Continue cooking gently for 10–15 minutes, until fragrant and pale gold in colour. Add couscous, stir well, then tip in hot stock. Bring to the boil, stirring, cover with a lid and turn off heat. Leave to infuse for 15 minutes. Before serving, stir through freshly chopped mint and vinegar.

2   Rub lamb with second measure of crushed coriander seeds and 2 tablespoons of olive oil. Grind on plenty of black pepper. Cook over a high heat on a barbecue hot plate or over a barbecue grill rack (or roast in the oven). Transfer to a plate, sprinkle generously with salt and leave to rest for 5 minutes before slicing thinly across grain of meat.

3   Put semi-dried tomatoes in a bowl with yellow pepper and olives. Mix dressing ingredients together, except parsley, and toss through salad. Just before serving, stir through fresh tomatoes and parsley.

4   Arrange couscous, salad and lamb on a large serving platter. Scatter over some more chopped mint and serve immediately.

NOTE
There are several cuts of lamb you can use in this recipe; here are some suggestions: 2 racks of lamb, trimmed, cut into mini racks of 3 cutlets each (cook for 10–12 minutes); 18 single cutlets (cook for 4–5 minutes); 3 lamb rumps about 180g each, trimmed (cook for 15–20 minutes); 8 lamb tenderloins, also known as lamb eye fillets, about 450g total (cook for 4–5 minutes). Allow meat to rest for a few minutes before serving and season with plenty of salt as soon as it comes off the barbecue.

Lamb cutlets with mustard & thyme

SERVES 4

These cutlets have been a Biuso family favourite for decades. You just can't go wrong with them – providing you buy good quality fresh lamb, that is. Serve with an aubergine dish of some sort, and salad and bread, or anything you like really – they're very accommodating.

2 racks young lamb
90ml olive oil
1 Tbsp creamy Dijon mustard
several sprigs thyme or lemon thyme
2 cloves garlic, peeled and sliced
salt and freshly ground black pepper

1   Remove fat coating on lamb if it is still attached. With the point of a small sharp knife, remove any silvery skin from meat and any other lumps of fat. Cut racks into cutlets with a sharp knife.

2   In a shallow dish, mix oil, mustard, thyme, garlic and plenty of pepper. Add cutlets and coat in marinade. Marinate cutlets for at least 15 minutes and up to 2 hours; bring cutlets to room temperature before cooking.

3   Cook over a very hot barbecue grill rack for 3–4 minutes each side or until crispy but still pink and moist inside. Transfer cutlets to a heated serving plate. Sprinkle generously with salt, then serve immediately.

Sticky chicken satay

SERVES 4 (MAKES ABOUT 30 SATAY)

Make a tangy and refreshing salad to go with these skewers using bean sprouts, chopped coriander leaves, cucumber, carrot strips, iceberg lettuce, lime juice, salt and pepper.

4 single skinned and boned chicken breasts,
** cut into strips**
1 Tbsp finely grated fresh ginger
freshly ground black pepper to taste
4 Tbsp soy sauce
2 Tbsp lemon juice
1 Tbsp runny honey
1 tsp crushed coriander seeds

bamboo skewers, soaked in cold water for 30 minutes

1   Thread strips of chicken breast onto skewers.

2   Mix ginger, pepper, soy sauce, lemon juice, honey and coriander seeds in a shallow rectangular dish. Add chicken skewers and coat in marinade. Cover with plastic food wrap and refrigerate for at least 2 hours, but up to 24 hours; bring to room temperature before cooking.

3   Cook over a barbecue grill rack or over a medium heat on an oiled barbecue hot plate (if barbecue is too hot, satay will stick), until golden and cooked through. Transfer to a plate and serve immediately.

BLAT baps

SERVES 4

Here's a twist on BLTs. A whiff of sizzling bacon in the air is hunger-inducing, but hot crisp bacon stuffed in a soft bap with some velvety avocado to soften its salty edge is just plain irresistible.

4 baps (soft bread buns) or use small pita pockets
8 rashers streaky bacon
1 ripe but firm avocado
small bunch cos or buttercrunch lettuce leaves
2 medium vine-ripened tomatoes, sliced
handful of young basil leaves
4 gherkins, patted dry and sliced
½ cup ready-made mayonnaise
freshly ground black pepper

1 Toast baps, let them cool, then cut in half through the middle. Cook bacon on barbecue hot plate or grill rack, or fry it in a little oil. Cut avocado in half, remove stone, then skin, and slice flesh thickly.

2 Layer bap bases with lettuce, tomatoes, basil, avocado, bacon, gherkins and mayonnaise. Grind over pepper, put bap tops on and serve immediately.

a whiff of sizzling bacon and

velvety avocado to soften its salty edge

Devilled chicken wings

SERVES 4

Be careful not to brown the chicken wings too quickly; it is best to cook them slowly and thoroughly. If liked, transfer the wings to the barbecue grill rack for the last few minutes. Add a stalk of rosemary to the heat source, fan the flames and let the wings absorb the rosemary smoke for a few seconds.

¼ cup extra virgin olive oil
1 tsp paprika
1 tsp ground cumin
finely grated zest of 1 lemon
freshly ground black pepper to taste
1kg chicken wings, halved
salt
lime wedges for serving

1   In a shallow dish mix oil, paprika, cumin, lemon zest and a good grinding of black pepper. Add chicken wings and turn to coat in dressing. Cover and marinate for at least 1 hour, but up to 24 hours, refrigerated, turning occasionally.

2   Gently turn chicken wings in dressing, adding ½ teaspoon of salt. Cook over a low to medium heat on an oiled barbecue hot plate for about 45 minutes or until cooked through and well coloured; baste with marinade juices from time to time. Alternatively, cook in an oven preheated to 180°C (set on fanbake) for about 25 minutes or until golden and cooked through.

3   Transfer chicken wings to a platter, sprinkle with salt and squeeze over lime wedges. Serve hottish or at room temperature as a nibble or as part of a barbecue meal.

fan the flames and

take in the rosemary scent...

Thai coconut chicken cakes

SERVES 4 (MAKES 30 SMALL CAKES)

These are simple and delicious. Don't shake the can of coconut cream, let it settle for as long as possible, then scoop off the rich cream from the top. Serve these with rice and a cucumber and mint salad.

CHICKEN CAKES
500g chicken mince
1 Tbsp red curry paste
2 Tbsp chopped coriander
3 Tbsp thick part of a can of coconut cream (see Glossary)
½ tsp salt
oil for frying

COCONUT SAUCE
1 fresh, juicy lime
120ml thick part of a can of coconut cream (see Glossary)
4 tiny dried bird's eye chillies, crushed
4 kaffir lime leaves

CHICKEN CAKES

1 Mix together all ingredients except oil. Roll mixture into marble-sized balls, and chill for 1–2 hours.

2 Cook chicken cakes over a medium heat on an oiled barbecue hot plate, flattening them a little to let them cook evenly, until browned and cooked through.

COCONUT SAUCE

1 Peel rind from lime using a small serrated knife, then cut in between membranes to release small pieces of lime fillet. Chop lime flesh into small pieces.

2 Put coconut cream, chillies and lime leaves in a small saucepan and simmer gently until reduced by about half. Add chopped lime and serve sauce with chicken cakes.

Beef kebabs with thyme & ginger

SERVES 6

These colourful beef kebabs have strong clear flavours of ginger and garlic and a lovely sweetness from the peppers and onions. Serve with crusty bread or fat fingers of crunchy potatoes and a salad.

1 kg scotch fillet
2 Tbsp olive oil
juice of 1 lemon
salt and freshly ground black pepper
several sprigs of fresh thyme
2 Tbsp freshly grated ginger
2 cloves garlic, peeled and crushed
1 red and 1 green pepper
(capsicum), cored, deseeded and
cut into chunks
2 large red onions, peeled and cut
into chunks
2 courgettes (zucchini), cut into
thick rounds

bamboo skewers, soaked for 30
minutes in cold water

1 Remove excess fat from meat and any silvery skin and cut into large cubes. For medium–rare cut into 2.5–3cm cubes. Cut into smaller cubes if meat is preferred medium. In a large shallow dish mix oil, lemon juice, 1¼ teaspoons of salt, plenty of black pepper, thyme, ginger and garlic. Add meat and coat with marinade. Cover and refrigerate for at least 2 hours, but up to 24 hours, turning often; stir occasionally.

2 Thread meat onto skewers alternating with pieces of pepper, onion and courgette.

3 Cook kebabs over a high heat on an oiled barbecue hot plate for about 7 minutes, turning often and basting with marinade.

...a grate of

ginger contrasts

with the lovely

sweetness of

peppers

Avocado, bacon & corn baps

SERVES 4

If you like bacon and avocado together, try this combination which includes freshly cooked sweet corn, lime juice, red onion and sweet chilli sauce. Yum! You could use smoked chicken breasts in place of bacon for a change.

2 fresh sweet corn cobs
250g streaky bacon
olive oil
**1 medium red onion, peeled and
  sliced**
1 large ripe but firm avocado
2 Tbsp fresh lime juice
salt and freshly ground black pepper
4 baps (soft bread buns)
**handful of cos lettuce or
  buttercrunch leaves**
**2 medium vine-ripened tomatoes,
  diced**
sweet chilli sauce of your choice
2 Tbsp chopped coriander

1 Remove husks and silks from corn cobs, then boil gently for about 12 minutes or until tender. Drain, then drape cobs with a large piece of absorbent kitchen paper until cool enough to handle.

2 Cook bacon on the barbecue hot plate or grill or fry it in a little hot oil. Set aside and keep warm.

3 Cook onion on an oiled barbecue hot plate for several minutes or until it is limp but not coloured, or cook in 1 tablespoon of oil in a small saucepan over a medium heat.

4 Using a large sharp knife, cut the kernels off the cobs. Cut avocado in half and remove stone. Peel, then slice flesh thickly. Sprinkle with lime juice and season with a little salt and pepper. Split baps in half through the middle.

5 Fill baps with lettuce, corn kernels, red onion, bacon, avocado, tomato, sweet chilli sauce and coriander. Serve immediately.

Sausages, mash & fried green tomatoes

SERVES 8

Fried green tomatoes make a superb accompaniment to sausages and mash because they're sweet and sharp, and crisp and juicy. This recipe for Fried Green Tomatoes comes from my Tuscan aunt Irene. She serves them in typical Tuscan style with sweet pork sausages flavoured with black pepper, and pillows of soft whipped potatoes. You'll need to order the tomatoes several days in advance from a greengrocer and start preparing them about 2 hours before you need to cook them.

Use floury potatoes for the mash, a type that is soft and fluffy when cooked, and beat in plenty of butter, salt and hot milk to turn them into a light fluffy purée.

FRIED GREEN TOMATOES

8 large unripe green tomatoes, washed and dried

salt

½ cup plain flour

extra virgin olive oil

12 top-quality pork sausages, cooked gently on the barbecue in time to serve with mash and tomatoes

POTATO MASH

1kg floury potatoes (see Glossary), peeled and cut into smallish, even-sized cubes

salt

1 cup milk

butter

1 Cut tomatoes into 1.5cm-thick slices and arrange on a wire cake rack. Sprinkle with salt, then turn them over and sprinkle the other side with salt. Leave to drain for 1 hour, then turn and drain for 1 hour further.

2 Cook potatoes in a saucepan in plenty of gently boiling, salted water until tender, about 15–20 minutes. Drain potatoes well and return to pan. Put pan back over heat for 30 seconds to drive off any clinging moisture. (Start the sausages on a gentle heat once the potatoes are under way.)

3 Mash potatoes with a hand masher or pass through a mouli-légumes. Heat milk until just under boiling point and mix into purée by degrees, along with a knob of butter and ½ teaspoon of salt. Beat well with a wooden spoon, adding enough milk to make potato light and fluffy. Check for salt, then transfer to a deep and solid china bowl and cover with a lid; the mash will stay good and hot for about 20 minutes.

4 Just prior to cooking the tomatoes, pat them very dry with absorbent kitchen paper. Sprinkle flour on a piece of paper (easy to throw out and saves washing a plate).

5 Pour oil to a depth of 1cm in a large heavy-based frying pan. Heat oil over a high heat. When it is shimmering and starting to haze, quickly coat about half the tomatoes with flour, then lower them into hot oil. Cook until golden on both sides, then remove with a slotted spatula, transferring them to a serving plate. Alternatively, cook the tomatoes over a medium heat on a well-oiled barbecue hot plate. Sprinkle with salt and serve with the sausages and mash while continuing to cook the rest of the tomatoes.

The big burger

SERVES 4 (MAKES 4)

The best way to serve burgers is to put all the ingredients on the table and let everyone assemble their own just as they like it.

BURGER PATTIES
1 tsp tomato concentrate
¼ cup tomato ketchup
1 small onion, peeled and finely chopped
1 Tbsp chopped parsley
salt and freshly ground black pepper
1 large gherkin, chopped
1 egg
500g prime minced beef
½ cup (30g) fresh white breadcrumbs
olive oil

4 iceberg lettuce leaves, torn into bite-sized pieces
½ cup grated cheddar cheese
2 tomatoes, sliced
2 gherkins, sliced
2–3 small canned beetroot, patted dry and sliced (optional)
2 hard-boiled eggs, sliced (optional)

4 burger buns, split in half
butter or mayonnaise
tomato ketchup
chutney of your choice

1 In a large bowl mix together tomato concentrate, ketchup, onion, parsley, 1 teaspoon of salt, plenty of black pepper, gherkin and egg, then beat in the minced meat and breadcrumbs.

2 Shape mixture into four patties, slightly larger than the buns. Stack patties, each separated by a layer of plastic food wrap, in a container and refrigerate until ready to cook.

3 Assemble salad filling ingredients. Cook patties over a medium heat on an oiled barbecue hot plate until browned and cooked through.

4 Toast buns and spread with butter or mayonnaise. Put some lettuce on each bun and top with a patty. Dribble on a little ketchup or spoon on some chutney, scatter over cheese and add a few slices of tomato, gherkin, beetroot and hard-boiled egg. Serve immediately.

Barbecued T-bone steaks with Dijon mustard

SERVES 4

I'd serve some sort of oven-baked crunchy potato dish with these steaks and a good salad of fresh leaves dressed with lemon juice, extra virgin olive oil, salt and pepper.

6 Tbsp olive oil
3 Tbsp creamy Dijon mustard
**salt and freshly ground black
pepper to taste**
4 aged T-bone beef steaks
salt

1 In a shallow dish mix together olive oil, mustard and plenty of black pepper. Add steaks and turn to coat on both sides with the mustard oil. Marinate for 30 minutes at room temperature, or for several hours, covered and refrigerated (bring to room temperature before cooking).

2 Cook steaks to medium-rare [see page 151] over very high heat on a barbecue hot plate; do not overcook them. Dish steaks onto a large heated plate or tray in a single layer and sprinkle both sides very generously with salt; do not stack them or they will steam as they rest. Let them rest for 5 minutes before serving so juices will settle.

NOTE
The T-bone has a piece of very tender fillet steak on one side of the T-shaped bone and a piece of tender sirloin on the other side. The strip of fat running along the side of the sirloin can be trimmed.

This is one of the most difficult steaks to cook well because the texture of the meat varies on each steak. The smaller piece of meat (the fillet) is more tender than the other piece (the sirloin), and the meat on both sides is thicker around the top of the bone where the bone is T-shaped. The bone also inhibits cooking. The flavour of T-bones cooked on the barbecue is superb, and if they are positioned so that the smaller piece of meat and the bone end are on the hottest part of the barbecue, they will be cooked at the same time as the larger, drier piece of meat.

Pork cutlets with fennel & bay leaves

SERVES 4

The most important thing with pork is not to overcook it. It should be cooked until the juices run clear, but the meat should still be a healthy pink. Once the juices run clear, remove meat from heat source or those juices will soon disappear and you'll be left with white tough pork. Serve these cutlets with new potatoes or a kumara (sweet potato) salad.

4 Tbsp extra virgin olive oil
1 stalk rosemary
1 tsp fennel seeds
8 fresh bay leaves
4 large cloves garlic, peeled and sliced
freshly ground black pepper
4 large pork cutlets
salt

1   In a shallow dish mix oil, rosemary, fennel seeds, bay leaves, garlic and plenty of black pepper. Add cutlets and coat with marinade. Cover and chill for several hours.

2   Bring cutlets to room temperature before cooking. Cook for 2–3 minutes on each side over a high heat on a barbecue hot plate, anointing with marinade during cooking. Finish off for 2–3 minutes more over a hot barbecue grill rack, fanning the flames a little so the cutlets take on a hint of smoke. Transfer to a serving plate, sprinkle with salt and rest cutlets for 5 minutes before serving.

3   Cook pieces of garlic from marinade on hot plate until golden, and transfer to serving plate as they are cooked.

Pork & fennel satay

SERVES 4–6 (MAKES 40 SMALL SKEWERS)

A great example of the sort of pork dish that you can quickly marinate early in the day, then put on skewers just before cooking. Serve with a salad of fresh sliced fennel with a lemony vinaigrette.

2 tsp freshly ground cumin seeds
2 tsp freshly ground fennel seeds
2 tsp turmeric
1½ tsp salt
1 Tbsp raw sugar
finely grated zest of 1 lemon
6 Tbsp thick part of a can of coconut cream (see Glossary)
700g trimmed pork (scotch fillet, steaks, etc), cut into small pieces
salad for serving

small bamboo skewers, soaked in cold water for 30 minutes

1   In a bowl mix together seeds, turmeric, salt, sugar and lemon zest. Blend in coconut cream, then add pork pieces. Stir well to coat pork. Cover and refrigerate for at least 1 hour, but up to 24 hours.

2   Thread meat onto bamboo skewers, about 3–4 pieces per skewer, not too tightly pressed together. Brush with a little oil then cook skewers over a high heat on a barbecue hot plate until crisp and brown and just cooked through.

Lamb & aubergine in pita pockets

SERVES 6 (MAKES 6)

Lamb and aubergine is a legendary success story. Stuffed into pita pockets and drizzled with a hummus and yoghurt sauce, then a dusting of spicy dukkah, it's even more moreish – you may just want two!

MEATBALLS
½ cup (30g) fresh white
  breadcrumbs
75ml water
750g prime minced lamb
2 eggs, lightly beaten
1½ tsp salt
1 small onion, peeled and finely
  chopped
1 tsp finely grated fresh ginger
1 clove garlic, peeled and crushed
1 tsp ground coriander seeds

1 medium eggplant (aubergine),
  sliced
olive oil
¾ cup ready-made hummus
¾ cup plain unsweetened yoghurt
6 large soft pita pockets
cos lettuce or iceberg lettuce, torn
  into bite-sized pieces
½ cup small mint leaves
¼ cup dukkah (ground mix of spices
  and nuts; choose a spicy one for
  this recipe)

1 Put crumbs in a large bowl and pour on water. Soak for 10 minutes, then add the rest of ingredients. Mix thoroughly with your hands and shape into 36 balls, each the size of a walnut in the shell. The meatballs can be cooked straight away, or covered with plastic food wrap and chilled for up to 12 hours before cooking.

2 Dunk aubergine slices in olive oil and cook over a high heat on a barbecue hot plate until well browned. Transfer aubergine slices to a plate as they are done.

3 Cook meatballs over a medium heat on an oiled barbecue hot plate, turning often, until they turn golden brown and are cooked through. Alternatively, heat 3 tablespoons of oil in a large frying pan over medium heat. Add meatballs and brown quickly on all sides (don't crowd the pan, cook in batches). Transfer to a plate as they are done.

4 In a bowl mix hummus and yoghurt until smooth. Wrap pita pockets in aluminium foil and warm them in a hot oven (or wrap in absorbent kitchen paper and warm them in a microwave). Cut pita pockets in half and split open. Fill pita pockets with lettuce, mint leaves, slices of cooked aubergine, meatballs, hummus dressing and a good sprinkling of dukkah. Serve immediately.

drizzle with hummus and yoghurt sauce...

and a dusting of spicy dukkah

Remo's butterflied leg of lamb with coriander & chilli

SERVES 6–8

This is my husband Remo's legendary lamb dish. In truth, it's my recipe, but he's developed a way of cooking it to juicy deliciousness – so all credit to him! The trick is to keep the heat slow and steady. If it is too high it will quickly blacken the lamb and prevent it from cooking properly through to the bone making it difficult to judge when it is cooked enough. The lamb will char somewhat, but keep the charring to a minimum.

1.5–2kg leg of lamb, butterflied
2–3cm knob fresh ginger, grated
juice of 1 lime
1 Tbsp runny honey
2 Tbsp oil
salt and freshly ground black
 pepper to taste
fresh limes and red chillies to
 garnish

DRESSING
2–3cm knob fresh ginger, grated
juice of 1 lime
½ tsp salt
1 Tbsp oil
2 tsp raw sugar
1 clove garlic, peeled and crushed
1–2 fresh hot red chillies, deseeded
 and very finely chopped
1 Tbsp each chopped mint,
 coriander and basil

1 Trim excess fat from meat but leave skin on.

2 Squeeze juice from grated ginger and put it in a large shallow dish. Mix in lime juice, honey, oil, 1½ teaspoons of salt and plenty of black pepper. Add lamb and coat with marinade. Cover and chill for at least 2 hours, but up to 24 hours, turning occasionally. Bring to room temperature before cooking.

3 Lift lamb out of marinade and pat dry with absorbent kitchen paper. Cook lamb over a medium heat on an oiled barbecue hot plate. Turn and baste meat from time to time. It will take about 40 minutes for medium–rare, and about 45–50 minutes for medium; if in doubt, slice through the thickest part to check. The lamb should be appetisingly charred, pink and juicy inside, wonderfully smoky, and, of course, scrumptious tasting! When lamb is ready, transfer it to a large plate and sprinkle generously with salt.

4 To make dressing, squeeze juice from grated ginger into a small bowl. Add lime juice, salt, oil, sugar, garlic and chilli. Just before serving, mix in the herbs.

5 Transfer lamb to a board. Slice meat across grain and arrange on a serving platter. Add meaty juices (but not any blood) from board and plate to the dressing then spoon dressing over slices. Garnish with a few slices of fresh lime and some chopped chilli. Alternatively, roast lamb in the oven. Heat 1 tablespoon of oil in a roasting tin in a very hot oven preheated to 220°C. Lift lamb out of marinade and pat dry with absorbent kitchen paper. Remove tin from oven and put in lamb, skin side uppermost. Roast for 45–60 minutes, basting once or twice with a little marinade.

Sausage & red pepper kebabs & melting mozzarella kebabs

SERVES 6 (MAKES 16 KEBABS)

To make rosemary stalks strong enough to use as skewers, choose thick stalks and leave them to dry for a day or two in the sun or at room temperature. Use a metal skewer to make an initial hole through the food, then slip the rosemary skewer through – that's much easier than trying to force a blunt stalk of rosemary through dense food!

200g (¾ of a small loaf) pide (flat
  Turkish bread)
150g bocconcini mozzarella, drained
  and patted dry
2 large red peppers (capsicums)
6 fresh chorizo sausages
dried rosemary stalks (to use as
  skewers)
3 large red onions
2 Tbsp extra virgin olive oil
1 Tbsp crushed coriander seeds
8 fresh bay leaves
freshly ground black pepper
oil

SALAD
4 cups trimmed rocket leaves
1 small cos lettuce, broken into
  bite-sized pieces
3 Tbsp extra virgin olive oil
2 cloves garlic, peeled and crushed
1½ Tbsp red wine vinegar
½ tsp salt
1 Tbsp creamy Dijon mustard
2 Tbsp capers, drained

small bamboo skewers, soaked in
  cold water for 30 minutes

1 Make up eight skewers of bread and mozzarella. Slice bread in half through the middle. Cut mozzarella balls into small cubes and cut bread to same size. Combine bread and cheese to make small 'sandwiches' (i.e. bread, mozzarella and bread). Spear carefully onto skewers.

2 Cut peppers in half, remove core and seeds, then cut each half into eighths. Slice each sausage into 5–6 pieces. Make up eight dried rosemary skewers with sausages and red peppers (use a metal skewer to make an initial hole through sausages and peppers, then pierce with rosemary stalks).

3 Peel and cut red onions into pieces through the roots. Mix in a bowl with extra virgin olive oil, coriander seeds, bay leaves and plenty of black pepper. Cook onions on a barbecue hot plate until lightly golden.

4 Cook the sausage and red pepper skewers first over medium heat on a lightly oiled barbecue hot plate. These will take about 20 minutes; don't hurry the process or you'll end up with raw sausage in the middle.

5 Once the sausage and pepper skewers are done, barbecue the bread and cheese skewers. Either cook them in the fat left on the hot plate or scrape it clean and oil it again (your call; but they take on a nice flavour from the sausages). Depending on the type of mozzarella, it will either melt very quickly, in which case you have to watch them very carefully, or it will melt more slowly and you'll be able to get the bread a good golden colour; in any event the kebabs will be delicious.

6 Arrange rocket and cos leaves on a large platter. In a small bowl whisk together oil, garlic, vinegar, salt and mustard. Add capers. Spoon cooked onions on to salad, and add dressing. Toss lightly. Top with kebabs. Serve immediately.

Pork satay with fresh pineapple chutney

SERVES 4 (MAKES ABOUT 20 SATAY)

This fresh chutney really lifts these satay to another level. If you don't eat it all in one sitting (but it's addictive, so you probably will), keep it refrigerated and use within 24 hours.

2 large pork fillets (750g in total)
small piece of lemon grass
2 cloves garlic, peeled and crushed
2 large shallots (about 100g), peeled and chopped
2 Tbsp lemon juice
3 Tbsp olive oil
1 tsp ground cumin
2 tsp ground coriander
2 tsp brown sugar
steamed rice for serving (optional)

bamboo skewers, soaked in cold water for 30 minutes

PINEAPPLE CHUTNEY
1 fresh pineapple
2 hot red chillies, deseeded and finely chopped
½ cup small mint leaves
1½ Tbsp lemon juice
1 tsp brown sugar
few pinches of salt

1 Remove and discard fat and any silverskin from pork fillets, then cut into small cubes. Thread meat onto bamboo skewers, 5–6 cubes per skewer, taking care not to press the cubes too closely together. Flatten the meat a little so the satay will lie flat on the barbecue. Put satay in a shallow dish.

2 Smash lemon grass with a mallet and put in the bowl of a food processor with the garlic, shallots, lemon juice and 1 tablespoon of olive oil. Blend to a paste. Add cumin, coriander and brown sugar, then pour this marinade over the satay. Marinate for 2 hours or longer, covered and refrigerated. Bring to room temperature before cooking.

3 Brush satay with oil and barbecue over a hot barbecue grill rack until cooked through. Serve immediately with Pineapple chutney and steamed rice.

PINEAPPLE CHUTNEY
1 Remove greenery from pineapple, then cut flesh into quarters lengthways. Slice off a little of the thick core from each quarter. Using a large knife, work it under the skin to remove skin and eyes. Cut pineapple quarters into wedges and put in a bowl.

2 Mix in remaining ingredients and taste for seasoning, adding more sugar, salt or lemon if required. Keep covered and refrigerate until ready to cook satay, then bring to room temperature.

Chicken kebabs

SERVES 4 (MAKES ABOUT 20 KEBABS)

Quick and easy – this is just the sort of thing to fling on the barbie mid-week. It is best to use a slow heat to start with to ensure the chicken gets cooked through to the centre, and to finish the cooking over a higher heat at the end to add colour.

2 skinned and boned chicken
   breasts (about 600g), trimmed
1 large red pepper (capsicum),
   deseeded and cubed
2 medium-sized red onions, peeled
   and cut into fat chunks through
   the root
8 fresh bay leaves
3 Tbsp extra virgin olive oil
1 Tbsp creamy Dijon mustard
1 tsp runny honey
finely grated zest of 1 lemon
2 Tbsp thyme leaves
pinch of chilli powder
salt and freshly ground black pepper
fluffy steamed rice for serving
   (optional)

bamboo skewers, soaked in cold
   water for 30 minutes

1 Cut chicken into large cubes and thread onto skewers alternating with pieces of red pepper, onion and the bay leaves.

2 In a large shallow dish mix oil, mustard, honey, lemon zest, thyme, chilli powder, and ½ teaspoon each of salt and freshly ground black pepper. Add chicken kebabs, and turn to coat in the marinade. Marinate for at least 30 minutes, but up to 24 hours, covered and refrigerated.

3 Cook kebabs over medium heat on an oiled barbecue hot plate, or under a preheated oven grill, until chicken is cooked through. Serve with fluffy steamed rice.

from the sea

Start with spanking fresh fish, or mussels, shiny and wet, or a clutch of coral-pink prawns. Add a squeeze of lime, a smattering of chilli and a swirl of coconut cream, and turn them into paradise on a plate.

above: mussels in lemon grass broth page 84
right: mussels on the hot plate

Seared fish with rocket & potato crush

SERVES 4

Potato crush (roughly mashed potatoes) makes an excellent base for lightly cooked barbecued fish, resulting in a light and delicious meal.

700g floury (late season) potatoes
(see Glossary) or small new
potatoes, scrubbed
salt and freshly ground black pepper
700g thick fish fillets (snapper,
halibut, monkfish, etc), rinsed,
patted dry and cut into 3–4 pieces
2 Tbsp olive oil
extra virgin olive oil
130g rocket leaves, trimmed
1 cup cherry tomatoes, halved
20 Kalamata olives, stoned
balsamic vinegar

1 Cook potatoes in gently boiling salted water until tender.

2 Put fish in a shallow dish and coat with olive oil. Sprinkle with salt and grind on a little black pepper. Cook fish quickly over medium heat on a barbecue hot plate until golden, then flip pieces and cook other side just to sear; fish should remain a little underdone because it will continue to cook as it stands.

3 When potatoes are tender, drain well and turn out onto a large platter. Crush with a fork, seasoning generously with salt, pepper and extra virgin olive oil. Add rocket and stir though.

4 Transfer fish to the platter on top of potato, scatter over tomatoes and olives and season with a little more salt and pepper. Serve immediately with balsamic vinegar for splashing.

crush potatoes, drizzle with oil...

and top with sizzling fish

Fish parcels with coconut cream & kaffir lime leaves

SERVES 4

There's nothing complicated here – just fresh, spicy flavours complemented by a creamy coconut sauce. The fish parcels can be prepared ahead, but keep them refrigerated and then bring to room temperature before cooking.

4 x 200g white fish fillets (snapper, red mullet or bream)
salt
125ml thick part of a can of coconut cream (see Glossary)
6 Tbsp red curry paste
4 kaffir lime leaves
4 Tbsp chopped coriander
steamed rice for serving

natural string for tying fish parcels

1 Cut four sheets of baking paper each 32cm long and spread out on the bench. (Alternatively, use sheets of double-thickness aluminium foil and oil the part that will come in contact with the fish.) Rinse fillets, shake dry, then put one on each sheet of baking paper. Fold fillets, tucking in thin parts to make parcels of an even thickness.

2 Sprinkle fish with salt and spoon over coconut cream. Put 1½ tablespoons of curry paste on each fillet, top with a kaffir lime leaf and a sprinkling of coriander.

3 Tie parcels firmly with string (tie in a bow; they'll be easy to undo later), allowing a little bit of room for ingredients to swell.

4 Cook fish parcels on a heated barbecue hot plate or in an oven preheated to 180°C (set on fanbake) for 15–20 minutes or until nearly cooked. Test for doneness by untying one of the parcels; be careful not to overcook fish, remembering that it will continue to cook as it stands.

5 Serve fish parcels with a bowl of steamed rice, and encourage everyone to add rice to their own fish parcel.

Fish masala

SERVES 4

Accompany this exotic fish stew with a huge bowl of steaming rice and serve with spoons.

MASALA
2½ tsp coriander seeds
1½ tsp cumin seeds
3cm piece ginger, finely grated
2 cloves garlic, peeled and chopped
1 tsp ground turmeric
¼ tsp chilli powder
¾ cup thick part of a can of coconut
    cream (see Glossary)
3 Tbsp vegetable oil
1 large onion, peeled and finely
    chopped
400g can tomatoes, mashed

750g monkfish, blue cod, or other
    white fish, rinsed and cubed
1 tsp salt
¼ cup chopped coriander
1 lime, quartered, for serving

1 Heat a dry frying pan over a medium heat and add coriander and cumin seeds. Cook for a few minutes, shaking pan until seeds smell fragrant and darken slightly. Transfer to a spice grinder and grind to a powder.

2 Put ginger, garlic, turmeric, chilli powder and coconut cream in the bowl of a food processor and process until blended.

3 Heat 2 tablespoons of the oil in a medium-sized frying pan over a medium heat and add onion. Cook until golden, then add spicy coconut cream mixture and ¾ cup water. Cook gently for 10 minutes until liquid in pan looks oily and smells very fragrant. Add tomatoes and bring to a gentle boil. Cook gently for 15 minutes, stirring often.

4 Put fish cubes in a shallow dish and drizzle with the remaining oil. Toss well. Cook fish over a medium heat on a barbecue hot plate until nearly cooked through. Add to pan with masala sauce. Season with salt, sprinkle with coriander and serve from the pan, garnished with lime wedges.

Coconut fish cakes

SERVES 6 (MAKES ABOUT 16 CAKES)

This is a great way to use up an excess of freshly caught fish. Cook the fish, eat what you want for the first meal then refrigerate the leftovers and turn them into these fish cakes the next day. Both the dressings are superb, so I usually serve some of each.

FISH CAKES

750g flaky white fish fillets, rinsed and patted dry

oil

¼ cup thick part of a can of coconut cream (see Glossary)

½ cup (40g) desiccated coconut

4 Tbsp fresh breadcrumbs (or a little more if necessary)

½ tsp salt

1 tsp raw sugar

2 Tbsp finely chopped coriander

2 Tbsp plain flour

1 egg

COCONUT DRESSING

4 tiny dried bird's eye chillies, crushed

120ml thick part of a can of coconut cream (see Glossary)

4 kaffir lime leaves

LIME DRESSING

1 fresh juicy lime

4 tiny dried bird's eye chillies, crushed

4 Tbsp extra virgin olive oil

4 kaffir lime leaves

1   Smear fish fillets with oil on both sides. Cook over a medium heat on a barbecue hot plate, carefully turning once with a fish slice, until nearly cooked through. Cool briefly, then flake with a fork and place in a bowl. Beat in the remaining ingredients. Shape into 16 or so fish cakes and refrigerate until ready to cook.

2   Cook fish cakes over a medium heat on an oiled barbecue hot plate until golden on both sides. Drain fish cakes briefly on absorbent kichen paper, then serve hot with dressing of choice. Alternatively, serve with a ready-made peanut sauce.

3   To make Coconut Dressing, put all ingredients in a small pan and simmer gently until reduced by about half. Set aside until ready to use.

4   To make Lime Dressing, peel rind from lime using a small serrated knife, then cut between membranes to release small pieces of lime fillet. Chop lime flesh into small pieces. In a small bowl combine remaining ingredients and add chopped lime, including any lime juice.

Whole fish with coriander

SERVES 4

A fish grill makes light work of turning over a whole fish on the barbecue.

1kg–1.2kg whole white fish, gutted and scaled
2 lime wedges plus extra for serving
3 Tbsp vegetable oil
2 Tbsp lime juice
2 cloves garlic, peeled and chopped
¾ tsp salt
3 Tbsp chopped coriander
3 Tbsp dried white breadcrumbs

1 Rinse fish inside and out, drain briefly, then pat dry with absorbent kitchen paper. Put lime wedges inside the cavity, then transfer fish to a large dish.

2 In a small bowl mix together oil, lime juice, garlic, salt and coriander. Pour this over the fish, cover and marinate for 1 hour in the fridge, turning once or twice. Remove fish from fridge 10 minutes before cooking.

3 Open up the fish grill, oil inside lightly and put fish inside. Sprinkle over half the crumbs and pat them on. Turn fish grill over and open up to sprinkle other side of fish with remaining crumbs. Close fish grill and secure clamp. Set fish grill about 10cm from a glowing bed of coals or over a preheated barbecue grill rack.

4 Cook fish over a medium heat for approximately 20 minutes, turning and basting once or twice. To check if fish is cooked, insert a knife into the meatiest part – the flesh should be pearly pinky-white all the way to the bone and the eyes will be white. Do not over-cook. When fish is ready, undo clamp on grill, fold back top part of grill and fold it under and carefully turn fish onto a serving plate. Serve immediately with extra lime wedges.

Fish fillets with tomatoes & lime

SERVES 6

I love this dish with a big bowl of fluffy fragrant rice. That's all it needs – and a glass or two of sauvignon blanc! The onion and tomato mixture can be cooked 1 hour ahead if need be, but the fish should be cooked just before serving.

3 Tbsp extra virgin olive oil
1 large onion, peeled and sliced
10 small vine-ripened tomatoes, halved
1 kg smallish white fish fillets, rinsed and patted dry
2 Tbsp olive oil
salt and freshly ground black pepper
3 Tbsp chopped coriander
3 Tbsp chopped mint
juice of 2 limes

1 Put extra virgin olive oil in a medium-sized frying pan and set over a low to medium heat. Add onion and cook gently until soft and translucent, about 10 minutes. Put tomatoes on top, cut side down, and cook for a further 5 minutes. Turn off the heat.

2 Cut each fish fillet in half through its natural division and put in a large bowl. Pour over olive oil and toss gently. Cook fillets over a medium heat on a barbecue hot plate for 2–3 minutes on each side.

3 Transfer fillets to a large platter as they are cooked and season with salt and pepper. Spoon cooked onion and tomato mixture over the fish. Sprinkle herbs over, then drizzle with lime juice. Serve immediately.

Fish kebabs with cherry tomatoes & lime pickle

SERVES 6

These juicy, fresh-tasting kebabs can be served with rice or couscous.

750g skinned gurnard fillets, or firm-textured fish that will hold together well, rinsed and patted dry
1 thin-skinned lemon
3 Tbsp olive oil
1 Tbsp chopped mint
salt and freshly ground black pepper
1½ cups small cherry tomatoes
32 fresh bay leaves
lime pickle for serving

bamboo skewers, soaked in cold water for 30 minutes

1   Cut fish into chunks. Peel lemon and cut rind into long thin strips. In a bowl mix together rind, oil, mint, ¼ teaspoon of salt, and pepper to taste. Add fish and stir gently to coat. Thread fish onto skewers, alternating chunks with cherry tomatoes and bay leaves.

2   Cook kebabs over medium heat on an oiled barbecue hot plate until fish is just cooked and lightly browned. Brush with marinade juices when necessary. Serve immediately with lime pickle.

a squirt of lime is all it needs...

Mussels in lemon grass broth

SERVES 6 AS A STARTER

If your barbecue has a wok attachment, use it to cook these mussels. Alternatively, cook them conventionally in a saucepan. Make sure the mussels are well scrubbed and soaked because the cooking juices form the sauce. If serving mussels more simply, cook them on a hot plate heated to medium until the shells open; splash with water from time to time.

1.5kg mussels

1 large piece lemon grass stalk, split and smashed with a mallet

small bunch coriander, roots attached

6 kaffir lime leaves, torn

2 Tbsp lime juice

2 hot red chillies, halved lengthways (flick out seeds for a milder heat)

2–3 shallots, peeled and finely chopped (¼ cup)

½ Tbsp fish sauce

½ cup thick part of a can of coconut cream (see Glossary)

2 spring onions, chopped

1 Scrub mussels under running water with a stiff brush, then pull off the beards. Transfer mussels to a large bowl filled with cold water. Stir mussels around, then lift them out into a clean bowl. Repeat process until water is clear and grit-free. Leave mussels to soak for 15 minutes in fresh water.

2 Put mussels in a wok (or a large saucepan) with lemon grass, washed coriander roots (chop leaves and set aside), kaffir lime leaves, lime juice, chillies, shallots and fish sauce. Cover with a lid and steam until mussels open. Transfer mussels to a large bowl, discarding any that have not opened.

3 Add coconut cream to wok. Bring broth nearly to boiling point. Stir through chopped spring onions and 2 tablespoons of chopped coriander leaves. Return mussels to wok, cover for 1 minute, then serve from wok or ladle contents of wok into a large serving bowl. Serve immediately.

Fish parcels with fennel

SERVES 4

Tie the string in a bow – it's easy to undo and take a peek to see if the fish is cooked.

4 x 150g white fish fillets (snapper, red mullet or bream)
bunch of spring onions, white part only, sliced
1 fennel bulb, trimmed and sliced
1 piece lemon grass, about 20cm, smashed with a mallet
1–2 hot red chillies, halved, deseeded and sliced
4 Tbsp roughly chopped coriander
salt
juice of ½ small lime
olive oil

natural string for tying fish parcels

1   Rinse fish fillets and pat dry with absorbent kitchen paper. Cut four pieces of baking paper each 32cm long and spread out on the bench. (Alternatively, use sheets of double-thickness aluminium foil and oil the part that will come in contact with the fish.) Put one fillet on the centre of each sheet of baking paper. Fold fillets, tucking in thin parts to make parcels of an even thickness. Scatter over spring onions, fennel, lemon grass, chillies and coriander. Sprinkle with a little salt, squeeze over lime juice and drizzle with olive oil.

2   Tie parcels firmly with string, allowing a little bit of room for ingredients to swell. Nestle each parcel in a piece of aluminium foil (it offers protection). Cook fish parcels over a low heat on the barbecue hot plate of a hooded barbecue with the lid down for 15–20 minutes or until fish is nearly cooked through. Alternatively, put parcels in an ovenproof dish and cook in an oven preheated to 180°C (set on fanbake) for about 15 minutes. Test for doneness by untying one of the parcels; be careful not to overcook fish, remembering that it will continue to cook as it stands.

Prawns with coconut & lime

SERVES 6

These prawns are sensational when served outside on a summer's evening as a pre-dinner nibble, washed down with icy beers.

6 limes
75ml thick part of a can of coconut cream (see Glossary)
3 small hot red chillies, halved, deseeded and
**   finely chopped**
8 fresh kaffir lime leaves
1 Tbsp freshly ground coriander seeds
30 large green (raw) prawns, thawed, rinsed and
**   patted dry**

1   Squeeze two of the limes and put the juice in a large bowl with the coconut cream, chillies, kaffir lime leaves, coriander seeds and prepared prawns. Toss well, slice the rest of the limes and add to the bowl and leave to marinate for 15 minutes.

2   Turn prawns and sliced limes on to the barbecue hot plate, heated to medium, reserving a little of the coconut juices to anoint prawns during cooking process. Cook until shells turn pink, turn them over and cook until just cooked through. Limes should be left on hot plate until well browned. Once the prawns and lime slices are cooked, transfer to a serving dish. Serve immediately with finger bowls of warm water and thick paper serviettes.

Fish parcels with shallots & tomatoes

SERVES 4

These are gorgeous to eat. Remember to undercook the fish because it continues to cook as it stands.

4 x 150g white fish fillets (snapper,
     red mullet or bream)
olive oil
salt and freshly ground black pepper
1 tsp ground coriander
4 black olives, stoned and chopped
1 Tbsp capers, drained
2–3 shallots, peeled and finely
     chopped (¼ cup)
1 clove garlic, peeled and sliced
4 semi-dried tomatoes, chopped
finely grated zest of 1 lemon
1 Tbsp lemon juice
1 Tbsp finely chopped flat-leaf
     parsley

natural string for tying fish parcels

1 Rinse fish fillets and pat dry with absorbent kitchen paper. Cut four pieces of baking paper each 32cm long and spread out on the bench. (Alternatively, use sheets of double-thickness aluminium foil and oil the part that will come in contact with the fish.) Put one fillet in the centre of each sheet of paper. Fold fillets, tucking in thin parts to make parcels of an even thickness. Season with salt and pepper and sprinkle over the ground coriander.

2 Combine olives, capers, shallots, garlic and tomatoes and divide between fillets. Top mixture with lemon zest and juice, parsley and a drizzle of oil.

3 Tie parcels firmly with string, allowing a little bit of room for ingredients to swell. Nestle each parcel in a piece of aluminium foil (it offers protection). Cook fish parcels over a low heat on the barbecue hot plate of a hooded barbecue with the lid down for 15–20 minutes or until fish is nearly cooked through. Alternatively, put parcels in an ovenproof dish and cook in an oven preheated to 180°C (set on fanbake) for about 15 minutes. Test for doneness by untying one of the parcels; be careful not to overcook fish, remembering that it will continue to cook as it stands. Serve immediately.

...untie the parcel and let the heady

scents waft up to you...

sides

Garlicky button mushrooms, golden crunchy potatoes, charred red peppers, stacks of glistening aubergine, tomatoes singed on red-hot coals . . . at the table side dishes should never be the poor cousin, but rather a glamorous aunt.

above: Charred red peppers with anchovies page 103
right: Norman's potatoes in the embers page 103

Charred courgettes with mint & vinegar

SERVES 6

Mint, vinegar and garlic are magic with courgettes. Serve these as an accompaniment to fish, lamb or chicken. Be aware that although the vinegar will mute the bright colours of the courgettes over time, the dish will still taste great. For a change, forgo the mint and vinegar and spread the charred courgettes with a little pesto.

500g (6 smallish) courgettes (zucchini)
2 Tbsp extra virgin olive oil
4 cloves garlic, peeled and very finely chopped
2 Tbsp finely chopped mint leaves
3 Tbsp red wine vinegar
sea salt and freshly ground black pepper

1   Trim courgettes and slice in half lengthways. Score cut surfaces with the point of a sharp knife. Rub courgettes all over with olive oil then cook over medium heat on a barbecue hot plate or grill rack until golden. Alternatively, cook in a ridged frying pan.

2   Transfer courgettes to a shallow serving platter and sprinkle them with garlic and mint. Splash with vinegar, season with salt and pepper and toss very gently. Serve at room temperature.

Colin's breakfast tomatoes

SERVES 6

My brother Colin does a pretty mean line in grilled tomatoes. This treatment captures their sweet fruity flavour – a deliciously perfect foil to a full-on breakfast of bacon, eggs, mushrooms and sausage.

6 large vine-ripened tomatoes
caster sugar
sea salt and freshly ground black pepper
¼ cup chopped basil or handful of tiny basil leaves
**   or 2 Tbsp thyme leaves**
butter

1   Halve the tomatoes and top each half with a pinch of sugar, a sprinkling of salt and a grind of pepper, a spoonful of chopped basil and a small knob of butter.

2   Cook tomatoes cut side down over low heat on a barbecue hot plate so that they warm though, but don't collapse. Increase the heat to high to brown them. Serve immediately. Alternatively, cook them skin side down first on a hot barbecue hot plate to char the skins, then turn them over and cook the cut sides until browned (in my book this is not as good because the tomatoes burst and lose their juices).

Escalivada

SERVES 6–10

The vegetables for this Catalan dish were traditionally cooked in the ashes of an open fire or barbecue pit, which gave them a delicious deep, smoky flavour. But the dish will still be a knockout if made with vegetables cooked on a barbecue grill rack or hot plate. For a spicy lift, season the escalivada with a jot of smoked paprika or smoked salt.

2 small or medium aubergines
  (eggplants)
olive oil
4 small red onions
1 bulb garlic
salt and freshly ground black pepper
12 very small new potatoes,
  scrubbed
2 red and 2 yellow peppers
  (capsicums)
2 slim fennel bulbs
4 small branches cherry tomatoes
lemon wedges
extra virgin olive oil (ideally from
  Catalonia if you can find it)
Spanish sherry vinegar
2 Tbsp coarsely chopped flat-leafed
  parsley
20 fat green olives (optional)
crusty bread for serving

TO COOK VEGETABLES IN HOT COALS

1 Rub aubergines with oil and put them on hot coals which are no longer glowing. Aubergines are very good like this. When they're tender, remove from coals, cut open and scoop out the smoky-tasting flesh (discard the outer skin).

2 Onions and garlic bulbs can go on whole. Remove onion skins after cooking and cut onions into wedges. Squish out garlic pulp and mix half of it into some mashed aubergine with salt and pepper. Potatoes are best oiled and salted and wrapped in aluminium foil (so the skin can be eaten). Peppers need to be done carefully so the skin chars without breaking the flesh and letting out the lovely juices.

3 Once vegetables have cooled peel off any charred skin, but do so over a dish to catch any juices (add them to dressing). Remove cores and seeds from peppers and tear flesh into chunks with your fingers.

4 Cook trimmed fennel bulbs whole, then peel off blackened parts before slicing or breaking apart.

5 To cook tomatoes, soak whole bunches of unskinned vine-ripened tomatoes (still on their branch) in cold water for 10 minutes. Put them on red-hot coals, greenery down. They will start to blister after a few minutes; turn carefully using long tongs and cook on other side for a few minutes. Fan coals to create a little smoke if necessary. Put tomatoes on a plate and cool. Remove skins, being careful not to rub any ash onto tomato flesh.

6 Arrange aubergine purée in a mound on a platter and top with lemon wedges. Add tomatoes to form a 'collapsed' mound and surround with other vegetables.

7   Squeeze remaining pulp from garlic bulb and put it in a bowl with 3 tablespoons of extra virgin olive oil and 2 tablespoons of sherry vinegar. Spoon this mixture over vegetables, sprinkle generously with salt and grind on loads of black pepper. Finally, garnish with parsley and olives if using. Serve extra oil and sherry vinegar at the table, along with crusty bread.

TO COOK VEGETABLES ON THE BARBECUE

Don't bother with potatoes, swap the cherry tomatoes for 6 or more Roma tomatoes, and use fresh garlic.

1   Cut the aubergines in half lengthways and score surface with the point of a sharp knife. Squeeze to extract excess liquid, then pat dry with absorbent kitchen paper. Rub with oil. Cook over a gentle heat on a barbecue hot plate, skin side down, until about half cooked. Transfer to the grill rack and cook on other side. When tender and well browned, transfer to a large platter (make a point of cooking aubergines thoroughly; if only half-cooked, they will be astringent and unpleasant to eat).

2   Halve peppers, remove cores and seeds and cut into strips. Peel onions, keeping root intact and cut into several pieces through the root. Mix pepper strips and onions in a bowl with a little oil. Cook over a medium heat on a barbecue hot plate until well browned. Transfer to a serving plate with the aubergines.

3   Cut Roma tomatoes in half lengthways. Coat with oil then cook for several minutes, cut side down, over a medium heat on a barbecue hot plate until browned. Add to serving plate.

4   Trim fennel and cut bulbs in half through the root, wash and shake dry (if bulbs are large, cut into quarters). Rub with oil and cook over a gentle heat on the barbecue hot plate to begin with, then increase heat and cook until tender.

5   Finish off Escalivada as described in cooking in hot coals, using freshly crushed garlic in place of roasted garlic purée in the dressing.

Button mushrooms with thyme

SERVES 6

You need really fresh mushrooms for this recipe – they should be as crisp as an apple.

500g very firm snow-white or brown button mushrooms, wiped clean and halved if large
4 Tbsp extra virgin olive oil
several sprigs thyme
8 small fresh bay leaves
finely grated zest of 1 lemon
salt and freshly ground black pepper

1   Put mushrooms in a bowl, pour on the oil and add thyme, bay leaves, lemon zest and pepper. Stir well to coat.

2   Cook on a very hot barbecue hot plate, turning often, until they are golden brown; don't overcook – they should be well browned but not soft. Transfer mushrooms to a side plate, toss through some salt and serve immediately.

Garlicky aubergine kebabs

MAKES 6 KEBABS

This is a quick and scrumptious treatment for aubergines. The trick is to ensure the aubergine cubes get thoroughly cooked without becoming too charred. If they're cooked too quickly, they'll blacken and taste bitter on the outside while remaining unpalatably raw in the centre.

1 large aubergine (eggplant)
salt and freshly ground black pepper
4 Tbsp olive oil
1 large clove garlic, peeled and crushed
1 tsp finely chopped marjoram or a few pinches of dried marjoram
lemon juice (optional)

bamboo skewers soaked in cold water for 30 minutes

1   Cut aubergine into large cubes, then thread onto bamboo skewers.

2   In a large shallow dish mix ¼ teaspoon of salt and plenty of black pepper with the oil, garlic and marjoram, then brush mixture over aubergine cubes.

3   Cook over a medium heat on a barbecue grill rack or on a hot plate, turning often and basting with the garlic marinade, until aubergine is crisp on the outside and very tender on the inside. Squirt over a little fresh lemon juice before serving.

Aubergine stack with asparagus

SERVES 4

This can be served as a starter, or as the main dish of a vegetarian meal, and it's also great with barbecued chicken or lamb.

500g plump asparagus, trimmed
olive oil
sea salt and freshly ground
   black pepper
2 medium-large aubergines
   (eggplants)
salt
3–4 large beefsteak tomatoes
handful of basil leaves
3 Tbsp extra virgin olive oil
aged balsamic vinegar
2 cloves garlic, peeled and crushed

1 Put asparagus in a flat dish, drizzle with olive oil and season with sea salt and pepper. Toss gently to coat spears with oil.

2 Cook asparagus over a hot barbecue grill rack for a few minutes on each side until lightly charred but crunchy, turning with tongs. Alternatively, cook in an oven preheated to 210°C until spears caramelise and tips turn crunchy. Asparagus can be cooked up to 2 hours ahead. Slice asparagus on the diagonal, reserving tips for garnishing. Split tips in half lengthways.

3 Slice aubergines into rounds. Dunk slices in olive oil and cook over a medium-high heat on a barbecue hot plate until very tender and a deep golden brown. Transfer to a plate and season with salt.

4 Cut tomatoes into thick slices, pat dry with absorbent kitchen paper and cook on a very hot oiled barbecue hot plate until lightly coloured; don't overcook. Arrange cooked tomatoes and aubergine in stacks, putting sliced asparagus and some of the basil leaves in between, on individual plates. Arrange asparagus spears on top.

5 Have ready a dressing made with the extra virgin olive oil, a few splashes of aged balsamic vinegar, garlic, ¼ teaspoon salt and some black pepper and torn basil leaves. Spoon over the stacks and serve immediately.

...a summery stack scented with basil

Couscous with chick peas & nuts

SERVES 6

Try this with simple barbecued meat dishes or as part of an all-vegetable meal.

2 yellow peppers (capsicums)

150g 'instant' (quick-cooking) couscous

200ml boiling water

1 tsp olive oil

50g unsalted cashews

35g flaked almonds

¼ tsp ground cumin seeds

¼ tsp ground cinnamon

½ tsp ground coriander seeds

100g cooked or canned chick peas

2 Tbsp raisins

salt and freshly ground black pepper

2 Tbsp lemon juice

2 Tbsp chopped flat-leaf parsley or coriander

2 Tbsp chopped mint

½ cup cherry tomatoes, halved (or quartered, if large)

1   Cook peppers over a medium heat on a barbecue grill rack until blackened, turning them with tongs. When outer skin is charred, transfer them to a plate and leave to cool. Peel off blackened skins, rinsing your hands as you do this, but don't put peppers under running water or you'll rinse away the flavour. Cut peppers in half, remove cores and seeds, reserving juices, and cut flesh into strips. Alternatively, cook peppers in the hot coals of a barbecue, or in the oven. To cook them in the oven, put peppers on a rack in an oven preheated to 200°C and cook for about 20 minutes or until peppers are blistered and charred. Transfer to a bowl, cover and when cool enough to handle, peel off blackened skins and discard cores and seeds. Chop peppers into strips and set aside with the juices. (Peppers can be roasted 1 day before required; cover and chill.)

2   Put couscous in a bowl and pour over boiling water. Stir once, then cover with a plate and leave for 10 minutes. Fluff up with a fork, cover again and cool.

3   Heat oil in a medium-sized frying pan over a medium heat and add nuts. Cook, stirring often, until lightly golden. Transfer nuts to a side plate.

4   Add spices to pan and cook, stirring, for 1 minute. Stir in chick peas and raisins and cook for 1–2 minutes until heated through. Season with salt and pepper and leave to cool.

5   Add lemon juice, parsley, mint, peppers and cherry tomatoes to couscous. Toss well. Stir through spicy chick pea mixture, garnish with nuts and serve.

Potatoes with Sicilian oregano

SERVES 4–6

Ideally, choose potatoes that are just a little bigger than a walnut in the shell. If the potatoes are bigger, cut them in half and make slits on the cut side. For a change use smoked salt or fresh marjoram in the potatoes.

salt and freshly ground black pepper
1½ Tbsp Sicilian dried oregano
1kg very small even-sized potatoes
2 Tbsp extra virgin olive oil
½ cup water

1   Mix ¾ teaspoon of salt, plenty of pepper and oregano on a plate. Make slits in the potatoes about three-quarters of the way through. Squeeze each potato to open the slit, pick up a little of the seasoning on a flat-bladed knife and smear it inside potato. Thread potatoes onto metal skewers going through the slit, not parallel with it, then put them in a shallow-sided ovenproof dish. Drizzle with 1 tablespoon of oil and add the water. Cover dish with aluminium foil and bake in an oven preheated to 180°C for 30–40 minutes or until tender.

2   Finish cooking potatoes over a medium heat on a barbecue hot plate adding a little extra oil if necessary. Sprinkle with a little more salt and serve hot.

Charred red peppers with anchovies

SERVES 4–8

Surprisingly, orange brings out the sweet, fruity flavour of peppers. If you don't have mandarin- or orange-infused oil, use lemon-infused oil, or extra virgin olive oil to which has been added the finely grated zest of 1 orange or 1 lemon.

4 red peppers (capsicums)
mandarin-infused extra virgin olive oil
250g cherry tomatoes
4 cloves garlic, peeled and crushed
handful of basil leaves
150g feta cheese, crumbled
salt and freshly ground black pepper
8 anchovies in olive oil, drained
2 Tbsp balsamic vinegar

1   Halve the peppers and remove seeds and soft membrane without disturbing the cores (cores will hold peppers together and stop filling spilling out). Rub peppers all over with mandarin-infused olive oil.

2   In a bowl mix together cherry tomatoes, garlic, basil, feta, and a little salt and pepper and spoon into the peppers. Top each with an anchovy and drizzle with a little balsamic vinegar and a tiny drizzle of the mandarin-infused oil.

3   Cook peppers over a medium heat on a double sheet of aluminium foil on a barbecue hot plate with the hood down for about 15 minutes or until peppers and contents are hot and starting to wilt a little and the bottom of the peppers are starting to char. If you have a top grill, flash peppers under it until crisp (or finish them off under an oven grill). Peppers can also be cooked in an oven preheated to 200°C for about 15 minutes (or until feta has browned on top).

Norman's potatoes in the embers

SERVES 6

My Irish friend Norman knows a thing or two about potatoes, and, like most men, he just loves building fires. He treats me to these potatoes once or twice each winter and it's a ritual I've come to love. Of course, building a fire is a bit of a performance, so these are not the sort of thing to whip up after a hard day's work. Make them the focus of a simple rustic meal with plenty of salad.

12 medium-sized floury potatoes (see Glossary)
sea salt
butter
freshly ground black pepper

1   Scrub potatoes and roll in sea salt. Wrap tightly in aluminum foil.

2   Have a good bed of hot embers ready. Bury potatoes in embers and cook for 30–45 minutes or until potatoes are tender when pierced with a fine skewer.

3   Serve with plenty of butter, sea salt and freshly ground black pepper.

Fennel on the barbecue

SERVES 4–6

Fennel cooked on the barbecue loses some of its aniseed power and ends up tasting something like globe artichokes – finger-licking delicious!

6 slim fennel bulbs
3 Tbsp extra virgin olive oil
2 Tbsp marjoram
salt and freshly ground black pepper
thick strips of lemon peel taken from 1 large lemon

1 Trim fennel bulbs and cut each one in half through the root, then wash and shake dry (if bulbs are large, cut them into quarters). Put fennel in a dish, add the oil then marjoram, salt to taste, black pepper and lemon rind. Use your hands to ensure fennel is well coated.

2 Cook fennel over a gentle heat on a barbecue hot plate to begin with. Increase heat once fennel has started to soften (after about 12 minutes), and cook until tender, spooning over a little marinade from time to time. Transfer to a barbecue grill rack, fan flames a little, and cook for a few minutes to colour and absorb a whiff of smoke (save the pieces of lemon rind from the marinade as they are delicious when cooked to a crisp on the barbecue hot plate). Transfer fennel and lemon rind to a plate, then grind on some pepper. Cool for 5 minutes before serving.

Baked potatoes, peppers & chorizo

SERVES 4

This colourful crunchy dish is a meal in itself – just add a few green leaves on the side. Or serve it alongside barbecue chicken or as part of a barbecued vegetable meal.

2 red and 2 yellow peppers (capsicums)
about 4–6 large floury potatoes (see Glossary), peeled and roughly cut into fat fingers
salt and freshly ground black pepper to taste
3 Tbsp extra virgin olive oil
3 fresh chorizo sausages
2 Tbsp fresh rosemary leaves

1 Halve peppers, remove cores and seeds and cut each half into three pieces. Put potatoes and peppers in a large shallow roasting tin. Season with salt and pepper and drizzle with oil.

2 Cook vegetables for about 1 hour in an oven preheated to 200°C, turning them over once or twice, or until golden and crisp.

3 Meanwhile, cook chorizo sausages over a medium heat on an oiled barbecue hot plate for a few minutes or until cooked through. Slice thickly, then add sausages along with the rosemary to the roasting dish containing potatoes and peppers. Cook for a further 5 minutes, then transfer to a serving dish. Serve hot.

crunchy potatoes and glistening peppers...

hard to resist

salads

A salad can be as simple as a bowl of immaculate crisp greens,

shimmering with oil, or as exotic as sweet juicy peaches and char-grilled

peppers with a brush of sea salt, chilli and toasted cumin seeds.

above: fresh leaf salad with Asian flavours page 114
right: red onions on the barbecue hot plate

Green tomato, avocado & orange salad

SERVES 4

Green tomatoes are as crisp as fresh-picked apples. In this salad they provide a counterpoint to the velvety texture of avocado. This salad makes an excellent accompaniment to simply barbecued fish or chicken.

2 medium-sized red onions
4½ Tbsp extra virgin olive oil
salt and freshly ground black pepper
4 oranges
2 Tbsp lime juice
1 tsp creamy Dijon mustard
2 cloves garlic, peeled and finely
   chopped
pinch of sugar
1 large perfectly ripe avocado
6 medium green tomatoes
¼ cup black olives, stoned
½ cup chopped coriander

1 Peel and cut red onions into pieces through the roots. Mix in a bowl with 1½ tablespoons of extra virgin olive oil and plenty of black pepper. Cook over a medium heat on a barbecue hot plate until lightly golden, then transfer to a plate.

2 Peel oranges with a serrated knife, removing and discarding all white pith, then slice into rounds. Put them in a bowl with any juice.

3 In a bowl mix the rest of the oil, lime juice, mustard, garlic and sugar with ½ teaspoon of salt and black pepper to taste.

4 Halve avocado, remove stone and slip off skin. Slice avocado flesh thickly. Slice tomatoes.

5 Arrange oranges, tomatoes, onions, avocado and olives in a salad bowl or on a platter. Scatter coriander over and pour dressing on. Toss gently and serve.

Avocado & tomato salad

This salad works with most barbecued meats, but try it stuffed into soft baps with crisp rashers of barbecued bacon.

2 perfectly ripe but firm avocados
1 Tbsp lemon juice
130g cos lettuce leaves or 1 small cos lettuce, washed, dried and torn into bite-sized pieces
1 cup cherry tomatoes, halved
salt and freshly ground black pepper
finely grated zest of 1 lemon
3 Tbsp extra virgin olive oil
½ cup small basil leaves
lemon wedges for serving

1   Halve avocados, remove stones and peel. Slice or chop avocado and sprinkle with lemon juice.

2   Arrange cos lettuce on a platter and top with avocado slices and cherry tomatoes. Season with salt and pepper, sprinkle lemon zest over and drizzle with oil. Scatter basil over and serve with lemon wedges.

Barbecued asparagus salad

SERVES 4–6

Serve this as a summer starter or alongside barbecued chicken, turkey or quail.

2 fresh sweet corn cobs
400g plump asparagus, trimmed
zest of 1 lemon
extra virgin olive oil spray or olive oil
1 cup cherry tomatoes, halved
1 Tbsp lime juice
½ cup basil leaves
salt and freshly ground black pepper

1   Remove husks and silks from corn cobs, then boil cobs gently for about 12 minutes or until tender. Drain, then drape cobs with a large piece of absorbent kitchen paper until cool enough to handle. Using a large sharp knife, cut the kernels off the cobs.

2   Put asparagus and lemon zest in a shallow dish and spray lightly with oil or drizzle with a little oil. Cook asparagus over a medium heat on a barbecue hot plate until lightly browned, but still crunchy.

3   Mix asparagus, corn kernels and tomatoes in a large bowl. Add lime juice, basil, a few pinches of salt and a good grinding of black pepper. Toss gently, then transfer to a serving bowl and serve.

Cucumber & peanut salad

SERVES 6–8

Biting and fresh, this is the perfect salad to sweep away richness from coconut-based barbecued dishes. If you want to make it ahead of time, get everything together but don't mix until the last minute.

½ cup raw peanuts
1 telegraph cucumber (long, tender-skinned cucumber)
1 tsp sugar
4 Tbsp white vinegar
2 hot red chillies, deseeded and finely chopped
2–3 shallots, peeled and finely chopped (¼ cup)
2 Tbsp chopped mint
fish sauce

1   Preheat oven to 200°C. Put peanuts in a shallow ovenproof dish. Roast for about 12 minutes or until browned. When cool, crush with a rolling pin or a mortar and pestle to make coarse pieces.

2   Trim and peel cucumber, slice in half lengthways and scoop out seeds with a teaspoon. Slice thinly and put in a bowl. Dissolve sugar in vinegar, pour over cucumber and toss well.

3   Scatter over chopped chilli, shallots and mint and toss well. Spoon on the peanuts, then sprinkle with a few drops of fish sauce. Serve immediately.

Tomato & cucumber salad

SERVES 4–6

Top this salad with a chunk of feta or crumble it over if you want to add a salty contrast.

1 small red onion
1 telegraph cucumber (long, tender-skinned cucumber)
   or 3 small Lebanese cucumbers
6 small vine-ripened tomatoes
1 green pepper (capsicum)
½ cup Kalamata olives, drained
salt and freshly ground black pepper
4 Tbsp extra virgin olive oil
1 Tbsp red wine vinegar
½ cup small basil leaves (optional)
1 small chunk of feta (optional)

1   Peel and slice onion into thin wedges. Soak in cold water for 15 minutes. Drain and pat dry.

2   Halve cucumber lengthways, remove seeds with a teaspoon and cut into thick slices. Cut tomatoes into quarters, removing cores. Halve green pepper, core and deseed and slice flesh into strips.

3   Put onion in a large bowl with cucumber, tomatoes, green pepper and olives. Sprinkle over ¼ teaspoon of salt and grind on plenty of pepper. Pour on oil and vinegar and toss carefully. Serve immediately, topped with basil leaves and/or feta if using.

Peach & roasted red pepper salad

SERVES 6

Hot spices and lemon zest dusted over a bowl of sweet roasted red peppers and juicy peaches is a real knock-out. Serve with barbecued duck, quail, pork, chicken or fish.

3 red peppers (capsicums), halved, cored, deseeded and cut into chunks
fruity-tasting extra virgin olive oil
¾ tsp cumin seeds
⅛ tsp chilli powder
1 tsp sea salt
finely grated zest of 1 lemon
4 perfectly ripe peaches

1   Put pepper chunks in a bowl and drizzle with oil. Toss well, ensuring every piece of pepper is coated in oil. Cook over a medium heat on a barbecue hot plate until softened and lightly charred. Alternatively, put peppers in a shallow roasting tin and drizzle with a little oil. Roast in an oven preheated to 180°C (set on fanbake) for about 30 minutes or until softened and lightly coloured around the edges.

2   Toast cumin seeds in a dry frying pan over a medium heat for a few minutes until they are fragrant. Grind seeds finely, then mix with chilli powder, salt and lemon zest.

3   Peel peaches only if skins are tough or bitter. Slice flesh. Transfer hot peppers to a serving bowl and top with peaches and all the juices. Sprinkle over spice mixture. Serve immediately.

Pepper & pineapple salad

SERVES 6

This is gorgeously sweet and juicy and goes well with barbecued chicken, pork, ham and duck.

2 red peppers (capsicums)
olive oil
1 fresh pineapple, peeled, cored, sliced and cut into chunks
2 Tbsp extra virgin olive oil
2 Tbsp lemon juice
½ cup small mint leaves
½ tsp freshly ground coriander seeds
salt and freshly ground black pepper

1   Halve, core and deseed the peppers, then cut them into fat chunks. Put pepper chunks in a bowl and drizzle with olive oil. Toss well to coat. Cook over a medium heat on a barbecue hot plate until softened and lightly charred.

2   Alternatively, cook whole peppers in the flame of a gas ring until blackened or cook them in the oven (see Couscous with chick peas & nuts, page 100). Transfer flamed or roasted peppers to a plate and peel when cool, removing blackened skin, and slipping out cores and seeds. Cut peppers into fat chunks, reserving any juices.

3   Put pineapple chunks in a serving bowl and arrange peppers on top.

4   In a small bowl mix together extra virgin olive oil, lemon juice, mint, ground coriander seeds, ¼ teaspoon of salt and plenty of pepper. Spoon over salad. Toss gently and serve.

Tessa's carrot & ginger salad

SERVES 4

This is excellent with spicy barbecued meats. The carrots must be fresh, sweet and snappy, not woody ones.

¼ cup lemon juice
¼ tsp salt, and freshly ground black pepper to taste
1½ Tbsp finely grated fresh ginger
1½ Tbsp chopped mint
4–5 carrots, peeled and grated

1   In a bowl blend together lemon juice, salt, black pepper, ginger and mint. Mix in carrots. Cover and chill until required.

...fresh green leaves

with a splash of lime

and a jot of

chilli...

Fresh leaf salad with Asian flavours

SERVES 4

This fresh-tasting salad is unbelievably good. The lettuce and herbs can be picked over ahead of time, washed and dried then kept crisp in an unsealed plastic bag in the refrigerator. Serve with seafood.

DRESSING
small knob fresh ginger, grated
2 large medium–hot red chillies, deseeded and sliced
2 cloves garlic, peeled and crushed
3 Tbsp palm sugar or 2½ Tbsp brown sugar
2 Tbsp fish sauce
4 Tbsp lime juice
2 Tbsp light oil
3 Tbsp dry white wine

SALAD
½ buttercrunch lettuce or tender green lettuce, torn into bite-sized pieces
1 cup each small mint leaves, coriander sprigs and Asian basil leaves
½ telegraph cucumber (long, tender-skinned cucumber), peeled and thinly sliced
1 cup fresh bean sprouts
2 spring onions, finely sliced

1   In a small bowl squeeze juice from grated ginger. Add rest of dressing ingredients, mix well and let stand for 15 minutes.

2   Prepare all lettuce leaves, herbs and vegetables and arrange on a platter.

3   Rewhisk dressing and taste; add more lime juice to make it sharper, sugar to sweeten it or fish sauce to season it. Pour dressing over salad, toss lightly and serve immediately.

Pink grapefruit & avocado salad

SERVES 4

Not only is this such a pretty salad, it also tastes fantastic. Serve it as a light starter or with barbecued chicken or pork.

1 tsp olive oil
¼ cup pine nuts
sea salt
3 pink grapefruit
1 Tbsp extra virgin olive oil
1 Tbsp manuka or fragrant honey,
    warmed
salt and freshly ground black pepper
1 ripe but firm avocado
130g bag cos lettuce leaves or
    1 small cos lettuce, washed, dried
    and torn into bite-sized pieces
mint leaves

1 Heat olive oil in a small frying pan or saucepan and add pine nuts. Cook, stirring often, until golden. Transfer to a plate lined with absorbent kitchen paper and sprinkle with sea salt.

2 Using a small serrated knife, peel grapefruit. Remove and discard pith. Cut flesh into segments, then squeeze juice into a small bowl.

3 Whisk extra virgin olive oil, honey and 1 tablespoon of grapefruit juice with ¼ teaspoon of salt and black pepper to taste (drink the rest of the juice!).

4 Halve avocado, remove stone, then peel and slice flesh. Arrange cos leaves on a serving platter and top with grapefruit segments, slices of avocado, mint leaves and pine nuts.

5 Rewhisk dressing and spoon it over salad. Serve immediately.

...sweet and sharp, crisp and velvety... the perfect salad

Quick Greek salad

SERVES 6

A handy recipe to have in your repertoire to serve alongside barbecued meats. If you can find small Lebanese cucumbers, use one in this salad in place of regular cucumber – they have a more delicate flavour.

½ small red onion, peeled and sliced

½ cup Kalamata olives, drained

3 vine-ripened tomatoes, cut into chunks

⅓ telegraph cucumber (long, tender-skinned cucumber), peeled and cut into wedges

130g cos lettuce leaves or 1 small cos lettuce, washed, dried and torn into bite-sized pieces

3 Tbsp extra virgin olive oil

1½ Tbsp red wine vinegar

salt and freshly ground black pepper

1 Tbsp chopped parsley

1 Tbsp chopped dill (optional)

100g feta cheese, crumbled (choose a dryish kind)

1 Soak onion in cold water for 15 minutes. Drain and pat dry.

2 Put olives, tomatoes, cucumber and onion in a large bowl with cos lettuce.

3 In a small bowl whisk together extra virgin olive oil and vinegar with ¼ teaspoon of salt and a good grinding of black pepper. Whisk in the herbs, then pour dressing over the salad. Toss gently, top with crumbled feta and serve.

salty, herby, sweet and juicy...

summer in a bowl

sauces & salsas

Little bowls of sauce and salsa, fruity, garlicky or pungent, pep up plainly cooked food and add layers of flavour to complex dishes. Have them on hand to inject even the simplest meal with a jot of sizzle and spice.

above: roasted hell-fire dip page 131
right: char-grilled chillies on the barbecue grill rack

Indonesian chilli tomato sauce

SERVES 6

Serve this fresh-tasting sauce with barbecued chicken, pork, lamb or seafood.

3 medium shallots, peeled and chopped (½ cup)
2 Tbsp kecap manis (Indonesian soy sauce) or dark
  soy sauce
1 large tomato, peeled, deseeded and chopped
2 Tbsp water
1 Tbsp lime juice
1 small hot red chilli, sliced
½ tsp sugar
½ tsp salt

1   Put all ingredients in the bowl of a food processor or in a liquidiser and process until smooth.

2   Store covered and refrigerated for up to 3 days.

Sweet 'n' hot dipping sauce

SERVES 6–8

Serve with fresh or barbecued fruit (pineapple, mango, banana, fresh or canned lychees), or chicken or pork satay.

1–2 hot red chillies, deseeded and finely chopped
2 Tbsp kecap manis (Indonesian soy sauce) or dark
  soy sauce
100g palm sugar (or dark brown sugar) finely shaved
  with a sharp knife
4 Tbsp lemon juice

1   In a small bowl stir all ingredients with a spoon until sugar is dissolved. Leave dressing to ripen for 2–3 hours, stirring occasionally, until it is clear. Adjust heat to taste, adding more chilli if desired.

2   Store covered and refrigerated for up to 3 days.

Spicy peanut sauce

SERVES 6

Serve with chicken, pork or lamb satay.

¼ cup peanut oil
1 onion, peeled and finely chopped
2 large cloves garlic, peeled and crushed
4 tiny dried bird's eye chillies, crushed
3–4cm knob fresh ginger, peeled and roughly chopped
175g roasted shelled peanuts
3 Tbsp kecap manis (Indonesian soy sauce) or dark
  soy sauce
1 Tbsp brown sugar
¾ cup hot water, or more to thin

1   Gently heat peanut oil in a frying pan. Add onion and fry for about 15 minutes until soft and a pale gold colour.

2   Add garlic, chillies and ginger. Cook for a few minutes, then tip into the bowl of a food processor or into a liquidiser. Add peanuts, soy sauce, sugar and ¼ cup of hot water. Process or liquidise until smooth, adding more hot water to bring it to a dipping consistency.

3   Store covered and refrigerated for up to 3 days.

Chillied plum sauce

MAKES 1 SMALL JARFUL

This is worthwhile making when plums are juicy and full flavoured. It can be made as hot or otherwise as you like by using hot chillies or by omitting them altogether. Try it with barbecued spare ribs, poultry cooked on the rotisserie or pork satay, and other barbecued meats.

600g red plums, peeled, stoned and chopped
½ cup caster sugar
½ cup cider vinegar
¼ cup water
3cm knob fresh ginger, peeled and finely grated
3–4 small red chillies, finely chopped and deseeded
  if preferred
½ tsp salt
½ tsp freshly ground black pepper

1   Place all ingredients in a medium-sized saucepan and stir until boiling. Turn heat to a simmer, half-cover pan and cook sauce until syrupy and thick, about 45 minutes. If sauce is very liquid keep cooking without lid until sufficiently reduced. If liked, purée sauce in a liquidiser or food processor.

2   Pour sauce into a clean jar or bowl, cover with a lid and refrigerate. Use within 4–5 days.

...when plums

are juicy and full

flavoured

Tahini sauce

SERVES 6–8

Tart and nutty, this sauce is particularly delicious with fish and lamb, but also good with barbecued chicken wings, thighs or breasts, and barbecued vegetables, especially aubergine, or with crudités (raw vegetables cut into sticks such as celery, carrot and red pepper).

2 cloves garlic, peeled and crushed
¼ tsp salt
½ tsp ground cumin
150ml tahini (sesame paste)
75ml lemon juice
about 75ml water

1   In a bowl mix together garlic, salt and ground cumin. Blend in tahini and lemon juice and beat until smooth. Add enough water to bring mixture to a smooth sauce consistency.

2   Store covered and refrigerated for up to 2 days.

Spicy tomato chutney

MAKES 750ML

Serve this chutney with avocado and taco chips as a pre-barbecue nibble. It also sits happily alongside barbecued chicken, lamb, turkey and pork dishes. It's sometimes just the thing to give a dish a welcome hot hit.

1 tsp cumin seeds
1 tsp coriander seeds
½ tsp fennel seeds
3–4cm knob fresh ginger, peeled and sliced
6 cloves garlic, peeled and chopped
400g granulated sugar
500ml white wine vinegar
½ tsp salt
½ tsp chilli powder
½ tsp garam masala
3 x 400g cans Italian tomatoes, mashed
100g golden raisins

1   Grind cumin, coriander and fennel seeds in a spice grinder or liquidiser. Add ginger and garlic and process to a paste. Set aside.

2   Put sugar and vinegar into a saucepan and dissolve sugar over a gentle heat. Add spice paste and remaining ingredients. Stir well, then bring to the boil. Turn heat to low and cook gently for 1½ hours, stirring often, or until mixture is shiny, thick and pulpy (during the last 15 minutes, stir often with a long-handled wooden spoon).

3   Ladle into a hot sterilised jar, or small jars, then run a clean knife through contents of jar to knock out any air bubbles. Cover with a damp cellophane jam cover and refrigerate when cool. Chutney will keep for many months, providing it is kept covered and refrigerated and the rim of the jar is kept clean.

Salsa verde

SERVES 8 OR MORE

This can give a real lift to simple dishes such as barbecued chicken or a platter of barbecued vegetables. It's also good with fish, pork and turkey.

1¼ cups finely ground fresh white breadcrumbs
2 Tbsp white wine vinegar
2 cups tightly packed parsley, stalks removed
¾ cup salted capers, soaked for 10 minutes in warm water, then drained (or use capers in brine; rinse well)
¼ tsp salt
2 cloves garlic, peeled and roughly chopped
1 tsp Dijon mustard
½ cup extra virgin olive oil or as required

1   Put breadcrumbs in a bowl, then pour in the vinegar. Leave to soak for 10 minutes.

2   Put parsley in the bowl of a food processor and process until finely chopped, then add to bowl of breadcrumbs. Next, in the food processor lightly process capers, salt, garlic, mustard and oil until mixture is coarse (don't process to a paste). Add to breadcrumb mixture. Blend together, adding more oil if necessary.

3   Store covered and refrigerated for up to 3 days.

Mango salsa

SERVES 6–8

Try this with barbecued chicken or lamb.

1 Tbsp extra virgin olive oil
¼ tsp salt and freshly ground black pepper
1 large perfectly ripe mango, peeled, stoned and
   finely diced
1 Tbsp chopped mint
3–4cm knob fresh ginger, peeled and roughly grated
½ small red onion, peeled and finely chopped
¼ tsp Tabasco sauce, or more to taste
1 Tbsp chopped coriander or parsley
1 Tbsp lemon juice

1   In a bowl gently mix together all the ingredients, taste and add more Tabasco if liked. The salsa is best used within 2 hours of making.

Golden salsa

SERVES 6–8

This is just the ticket with whole barbecued fish and fish kebabs. Use the same day.

1 Tbsp runny honey
juice of 1 lime
2 hot red chillies, halved, deseeded and very finely
   chopped
2 Tbsp shredded lemon- or lime-scented basil, or mint
6 golden kiwifruit, peeled and finely chopped

1   In a bowl mix together honey, lime juice, chillies and shredded basil or mint. Add golden kiwifruit. Marinate for 30 minutes before serving.

Tomato ancho salsa

SERVES 6

The ancho chilli, a dried red poblano chilli, has a sweet, mild and fruity flavour that teams up well with tomatoes to make a rich fruity salsa. The ancho chilli is often toasted before soaking, but it doesn't require that treatment in this recipe.

½ dried ancho chilli
2 medium–large vine-ripened tomatoes
2 cloves garlic, unpeeled
salt
juice of 2 limes

1   Soak ancho chilli in hot water for 2 hours or until soft. Drain well. (You may like to soak the whole chilli and use the other half in another recipe, and you can decide whether to include the seeds or not.)

2   Blacken tomatoes and garlic in the embers of a barbecue or over a gas flame. Start with tomatoes and put them right in the embers or the flame of a gas element. Turn with tongs as they blacken, then transfer to a plate as they are done. Spear garlic cloves on metal skewers and cook them over the embers or flame until the papery skin turns a deep brown. Cool.

3   Remove most of the blackened skin from tomatoes (a little charring gives the sauce its customary bitter edge), cut into quarters, cut out the cores and flick out the seeds.

4   Peel garlic and chop coarsely, then crush in a mortar with a pestle, adding a few pinches of salt (crushing it draws out the intense flavour). Add drained ancho chilli and crush to a paste. Finally, add tomatoes and crush to a lumpy salsa. Stir in 1 tablespoon of lime juice, then taste and add a little more if it needs sharpening.

5   Store covered and refrigerated for up to 2 days.

Quick lime mayonnaise

MAKES 300ML MAYONNAISE

A perfect accompaniment to a platter of barbecued prawns or with crabs, scampi or lobster. It's also excellent with char-grilled asparagus, and rotisserie chicken with baby potatoes on the side. For a change, substitute lemon for lime.

1 whole egg and 2 egg yolks, at room temperature
salt
250ml olive oil
finely grated zest of 2 limes
juice of 1–2 limes

1   Put whole egg and egg yolks in the bowl of a food processor. Add ¼ teaspoon of salt and whiz together briefly. With machine running, slowly dribble in oil through the feed tube. When all the oil has been added, transfer mayonnaise to a bowl, add lime zest and enough juice to give it a sharpish edge, but not too much to make it runny. Add more salt if necessary.

2   Cover mayonnaise with plastic food wrap and refrigerate until required. The mayonnaise will keep fresh, refrigerated, for up to 3 days.

Chermoula dressing

SERVES 6

This is excellent with barbecued fish and shellfish.

½ cup tightly packed chopped coriander
½ cup tightly packed chopped flat-leaf parsley
3 cloves garlic, peeled and roughly chopped
3 Tbsp lemon juice
2 tsp ground cumin
½ tsp paprika
½ tsp chilli powder
¼ tsp ground cinnamon
½ tsp salt
½ cup extra virgin olive oil

1   Put everything, except the oil, in the bowl of a food processor and blend until smooth. With the machine running, pour in oil. Transfer to a bowl, taste and adjust seasoning if necessary.

2   Store covered and refrigerated for up to 2 days.

Roasted hell-fire dip

SERVES 6–8

Offering a good hot bite, this dip is excellent served with barbecued aubergine, or barbecued beef, pork or chicken. Alternatively, serve it with shellfish such as prawns, scampi, scallops or crayfish.

2 large red peppers (capsicums)
3 slices white bread, crusts removed and cubed
¼ cup milk
¼ cup pitted green olives (or use pimiento-stuffed olives)
1 clove garlic, peeled and chopped
2 Tbsp olive oil
1 Tbsp lemon juice
1 tsp Tabasco sauce
finely chopped parsley to garnish

1   Char-grill peppers on the barbecue, in a gas flame, or in the oven (see Couscous with chick peas & nuts, Step 1, page 100). Chop coarsely.

2   Put bread cubes in a bowl and pour in the milk. Leave to soak for 10 minutes.

3   Combine red peppers, soaked bread, olives and garlic in the bowl of a food processor and process until coarsely chopped. Add oil, lemon juice and Tabasco sauce and process for 5 seconds. Turn dip into a bowl, cover and refrigerate for 1 hour before using.

4   Store covered and refrigerated for up to 2 days. Garnish with parsley before serving.

Pineapple salsa

SERVES 4

For a mild bite, use just 1 chilli. But if it's heat you're after, pep it up with more chillies. Try and find the sweetest and juiciest pineapple because it's the combination of sweet and hot that brings this salsa alive. Use the same day.

SALSA
2–4 long, mild red chillies
½ pineapple, skin and core removed, and cut into bite-sized pieces
1 tsp caster sugar
finely grated zest and juice of 1 lime
½ cup small mint leaves
1 Tbsp olive oil
3 Tbsp pineapple juice
salt

1   Prick chillies in several places with a fine skewer and either cook on a barbecue grill rack until blackened or toast over a gas flame. Wrap in absorbent kitchen paper, then peel and deseed when cool. Chop finely.

2   Put chopped chillies in a bowl with pineapple, sugar, lime zest and juice. Chop mint and add along with oil, pineapple juice and a few pinches of salt. Gently toss together, then serve.

sweetest, juiciest pineapple

...pep it up with chillies

sweet
endings

Smooth, rich and creamy, or cooling, fruity and good-for-you: sweet endings should embrace all these things. Drown scoops of ice cream in piping-hot espresso for the ultimate drop-dead-simple and decadent finale.

above: dried fruits cooked in paper page 134
right: glazed pineapple page 134

Glazed pineapple

SERVES 4–8

The sight of barbecued pineapple with a caramelised glaze makes me think of summer, no matter what time of year it is. But sugary fruits make a right mess of the barbecue hot plate. Fortunately, it's easily removed with water. Squirt plenty of water on the plate while it is still hot, scrape it clean, wipe with an old towel and it'll be just like new.

1 firm but ripe pineapple, peeled, cut into thick rounds, then into quarters
½–1 cup demerara sugar
vanilla ice cream for serving

bamboo skewers, soaked in cold water for 30 minutes

1   Thread pineapple pieces onto bamboo skewers. (Threading pineapple onto bamboo skewers is easier if you pierce the pieces with a metal skewer first.)

2   Put sugar on a large plate and turn skewers in it to coat. Cook over a medium heat on a barbecue hot plate until lightly browned (the hot plate should be clean but not oiled – the juice will soon run out of the pineapple as it heats). Transfer to a plate and serve with ice cream.

3   Alternatively, cut the pineapple into eighths, coat in sugar, then cook on a barbecue hot plate.

Dried fruits cooked in paper

SERVES 4

These fruit parcels are unbelievably good; plump and juicy and reeking of sherry! Serve them with cream or crème anglaise (proper custard which you can buy ready-made).

1 cup pitted prunes
1 cup dried apricots
½ cup dried apples
¼ cup dried cranberries (craisins)
6 dried figs, trimmed and halved
4 strips lemon peel
2 Tbsp cream sherry
½ cup water
2 Tbsp caster sugar
1 cinnamon stick, broken into pieces

natural string for tying parcels

1   In a large bowl mix together all ingredients and steep for 4 hours.

2   Divide fruit and cinnamon stick pieces between four large pieces of baking paper. Gather up corners of paper and tie with string. Nestle each parcel on a double piece of aluminium foil (it offers protection).

2   Cook parcels over a low heat on a barbecue hot plate of a hooded barbecue with the lid down for about 10 minutes or until they start to bubble. Alternatively, put parcels in a shallow roasting dish and cook in an oven preheated to 180°C (set on fanbake) for 15 minutes. Serve warm.

Minted lemon granita

SERVES 8

So you've over-indulged in salty, rich food on the barbecue … here is the perfect antidote, but you'll need to get it ready in advance! The liquid will take about 4 hours to start forming ice crystals, and will need occasional attention (to break up the ice crystals about every 30 minutes) for the next 2–3 hours.

pared rind and strained juice of 6 tart lemons
1 litre cold water
175g granulated sugar
40 mint leaves, washed
1 egg white
mint sprigs or extra lemon rind to garnish

1   Use a potato peeler to peel thin strips of lemon rind off lemons without removing any bitter white pith. Place water in a saucepan with lemon rind and sugar. Heat gently until sugar dissolves, then bring mixture to the boil, removing any scum from the surface. Boil briskly for 5 minutes. Take pan off heat and add mint leaves and lemon juice. Leave mixture to infuse for 15 minutes, then strain into a clean, shallow glass or china dish.

2   Place in freezer and partially freeze. Remove granita from freezer and using a fork break any set pieces into flakes. Return granita to freezer and repeat procedure every 30 minutes, breaking up ice crystals and returning it to the freezer several times until granita has the consistency of loose, frothy ice crystals.

3   Whisk egg white until it is just holding its shape, then blend it into the granita. Serve in chilled glasses (place in freezer for 30 minutes before filling) and top each with a sprig of fresh mint or twirl of lemon rind.

Fluffy pancakes with maple syrup

MAKES 20 PANCAKES

Served hot and fluffy with whipped butter and maple syrup or yoghurt and berries, these make a special brunch treat.

2 cups (280g) plain flour
pinch of salt
1½ tsp baking powder
2 tsp caster sugar
2 large eggs
500ml buttermilk
½ tsp vanilla extract
2 Tbsp melted butter

TO SERVE
soft butter, whipped with a wooden spoon
maple syrup

1   In a bowl sift flour, salt, baking powder and sugar. Separate eggs, putting whites in a clean grease-free bowl. Put buttermilk in a jug with egg yolks and vanilla extract and whisk together. Add butter.

2   Beat egg whites until just stiff. Pour buttermilk mixture into dry ingredients and stir just until mixed. Fold in egg whites.

3   Drop tablespoonfuls of mixture onto a medium–hot oiled barbecue hot plate spreading mixture a little with a spoon (so pancake is about 8cm in diameter). Cook until golden brown underneath. Flip pancakes over and cook other side until golden. Keep warm on a plate covered with a clean tea towel while cooking the remaining pancakes. Serve warm with soft butter and maple syrup.

4   Alternatively, cook pancakes 4 at a time in a large non-stick frying pan over a medium heat.

Jenny's caramelised bananas

SERVES 6

I only eat a big breakfast cook-up on the barbie when someone cooks it for me (not that I'm lazy…). My sister-in-law's bananas are delicious with crispy bacon, French toast and maple syrup – and taste even better when she cooks them!

6 firm, but not green bananas

1   Don't peel the bananas. Cut them in half lengthways and cook them, cut side facing up, over a medium heat on a lightly oiled barbecue hot plate until they show signs of softening.

2   Carefully turn them over and cook until lightly caramelised. Serve immediately in the skin.

3   Alternatively, if you like firmer bananas, cook briefly skin side down, then again cut side down on a hot barbecue plate until they turn golden brown.

Banana pikelets

SERVES 4–6

I can't decide whether these are best with lemon juice and sugar, melted butter and lemon juice and sugar, maple syrup and lemon juice or maple syrup and lemon juice and melted butter, so I usually end up having one of each!

1½ cups (210g) plain flour
¼ tsp salt
1 tsp baking powder
1 tsp baking soda
1 large ripe banana
½ cup (115g) caster sugar
1 egg
1 cup milk
1 Tbsp melted butter

TO SERVE
lemons for squeezing over pikelets
caster sugar
softened butter
maple syrup

1   In a bowl sift flour, salt, baking powder and baking soda. Make a well in the centre.

2   In a separate bowl mash banana and add sugar, egg and milk. Gradually blend banana mixture into dry ingredients, adding melted butter last.

3   Cook in tablespoonfuls over a medium heat on a lightly oiled barbecue hot plate. When bubbles form on the top, flip over and cook on other side. Keep warm on a plate covered with a clean tea towel while cooking the remaining pikelets. Serve with toppings of your choice. Alternatively, cook pikelets in a lightly greased frying pan set over a medium heat.

Caramelised fruit kebabs

ALLOW 3 SKEWERS PER PERSON

These kebabs look stunning and taste terrific. They're easily cooked in a grid pan, or heavy frying pan, or more carefully over a hot barbecue. They're seriously good served with a slice of freshly made cream-filled sponge cake or scoops of creamy vanilla-flecked ice cream.

FRUIT
choose from any combination
of bananas, kiwifruit, pineapple,
peaches, nectarines or
strawberries or other firm fruits
Cointreau liqueur or a liqueur or
spirit of your choice
icing sugar
butter

bamboo skewers, soaked in cold
water for 30 minutes

1   Prepare fruit by peeling, hulling or deseeding as appropriate, then cut into small chunks. Thread fruit onto skewers, placing them on a plate as they are done. Sprinkle over a little liqueur and leave to macerate for 10 minutes, turning from time to time. Sieve a little icing sugar onto a plate.

2   Heat the barbecue to medium-high and when ready to cook the fruit, butter the hot plate. Quickly pass kebabs through the icing sugar then put them on the hot plate. Cook for 1–2 minutes on each side or until the sugar is slightly caramelised. Serve immediately. (See introduction to Glazed pineapple, page 134, for tip to clean barbecue hot plate.)

3   Alternatively, heat a non-stick frying pan large enough to accommodate skewers over a medium heat. When it is hot drop in a little butter, which should sizzle and foam but not burn. Add the kebabs and cook until caramelised. Serve immediately. (Pour water into pan to lift off caramelised sugar.)

shiny and glazed...

splashed with liqueur

Blueberry buttermilk pancakes

MAKES 16–20 PANCAKES

Kids love pancakes – and so do adults! Make them for a late weekend breakfast, but rope the kids in to doing the work!

4 medium eggs
2 cups buttermilk
100g butter, melted and cooled
2½ cups (350g) self-raising flour
5 Tbsp caster sugar
finely grated zest of 2 lemons and
 juice of 1 lemon
400g fresh or frozen blueberries
Greek yoghurt for serving

1   In a large bowl whisk together eggs and buttermilk, then whisk in cooled butter. Sift in flour and stir in 4 tablespoons of the sugar. Fold in lemon zest and 300g of blueberries; don't stir because this will turn the batter blue.

3   Cook pancakes over a medium heat on a lightly oiled barbecue hot plate until golden brown. Flip them over and cook other side until golden. Keep them warm on a plate covered with a clean tea towel while cooking remaining pancakes.

4   Alternatively, heat a large non-stick frying pan over a medium heat. Lightly oil pan. Add tablespoonfuls of batter, spreading it out slightly, leaving enough room for pancakes to spread (cook in batches of three). Cook for 3–4 minutes or until pancakes are golden brown underneath. Turn pancakes over with a spatula and cook other side until light brown.

5   Put remaining blueberries in a saucepan with 1 tablespoon of sugar and the juice of 1 lemon. Cook gently for about 2–3 minutes. Serve pancakes with blueberry syrup and Greek yoghurt.

topped with tangy blueberries

Summer fruit parcels

SERVES 4

These are so good to eat, and so good for you!

1 mango
2 plums
2 nectarines
1 firmish banana
2 passionfruit or 2 Tbsp lemon juice
½ tsp vanilla extract
2 tsp runny honey
¼ cup shredded coconut, toasted

natural string for tying parcels

1   Peel mango and slice off both 'cheeks' (the two fleshy sides), then cut off any remaining flesh. Chop flesh and put it in a bowl. Halve plums and nectarines, remove stones and chop flesh. Add to bowl with sliced banana, passionfruit or lemon juice, vanilla extract and honey.

2   Put coconut in a small dry frying pan and toast over a gentle heat.

3   Divide fruit between four large pieces of baking paper and sprinkle the coconut over. Gather up corners of paper and tie with string. Nestle each parcel on a double piece of aluminium foil (it offers protection).

4   Cook parcels over a low heat on a barbecue hot plate of a hooded barbecue with the lid down for about 10 minutes or until they start to bubble. Alternatively, put parcels in a shallow roasting dish and cook in an oven preheated to 180°C (set on fanbake) for 15 minutes or until fruit is hot and steaming.

L'affogato al caffe

SERVES 8 OR MORE

This is so simple, but so delicious! When piping hot espresso is poured over ice cream, it melts into a rich, thick sweet cream around the edges, making an amazing contrast with the bitter bite of the hot coffee. Just the thing to finish off a special barbecue dinner. Yum!

creamy vanilla ice cream made with real vanilla pods
freshly made unsweetened espresso coffee

1   Put as much ice cream as you dare in small bowls or espresso coffee cups. Pour piping hot coffee over the ice cream and serve immediately with spoons.

barbecue know-how

Choosing a barbecue

It's impossible to recommend any one type of barbecue over another. More often than not, it comes down to what you've got, what's available at the time or what you've inherited. If you're looking to buy a new barbecue, consider the following:

Size *is* important. As barbecue activity is often at the centre of a social gathering, you might find yourself cooking for more than just your family. Make sure the barbecue you choose is big enough to comfortably cook extra food when the need arises. There should also be plenty of room to turn food and enough room where you can put food if it flares up or starts cooking too quickly, usually in the cooler areas around the edges. Small barbecues can get awfully crowded, and then they don't function well. If buying a gas barbecue, a three-burner barbecue is the best because you can cook keeping one burner on high, one on medium and one on low, and have the freedom to move food around according to how it is cooking. On those occasions when you're just cooking for two, you don't need to light all three burners so there is no waste of fuel.

If you're buying a portable barbecue, make sure the barbecue is steady – flimsy barbecues with wobbly legs are dangerous.

The rest is up to you and what you can afford: be it a basic barbecue or a state-of-the-art stainless steel kitchen-on-wheels, or anything in between!

Wood-fired barbecues

Devotees of wood-fired barbecues, which are generally purpose-built and not portable, claim they produce the best-tasting barbecued food. While it's true that the smoke from the wood imparts a distinctive flavour to food, this can be replicated in most types of barbecue by adding small amounts of tree twigs to charcoal ashes or by placing woody-stemmed herbs such as rosemary and thyme on lava rocks on gas barbecues. It really comes down to how you feel about *fire*. For some, a barbecue is not the real thing unless a fire is involved. This can mean collecting or drying off wood, cutting it into kindling, lighting the fire and waiting for it to burn down to ashes. It's not quick. (Wood and charcoal take around 45–60 minutes to burn down to embers. The flames should have died down and the embers or coals should be reduced to grey ash or glow red in the dark before you start to cook over them.)

This is the way barbecues used to be, and the smell of the smoke was a tantalising draw-card for miles around. I think this kind of barbecue still has a place, but it's more of an event than a quick way of cooking the evening meal. Summer and smoke seem to go together, and during summer holidays when everyone generally has a little more time, lighting a fire and waiting for it to burn down is an activity that most of us enjoy. It also keeps us outside, which is where we want to be in warmer weather.

Although most of the food is cooked *above* the embers, some items, such as potatoes wrapped in foil (see Norman's potatoes in the embers on page 103 and Escalivada on page 94), are cooked *in* the embers or directly *on* them.

Charcoal-burning barbecues

Fixed or portable, this kind of barbecue uses charcoal, which is clean burning and holds its heat for a long time. Charcoal can also be used in purpose-built wood-fired barbecues when wood is not available. While you can use firelighters to get charcoal started, never use petrol – it's dangerous *and* toxic.

Treat charcoal the same way as wood, i.e. wait until the charcoal burns down to embers before cooking the food. If you need to add more charcoal to the embers to bolster the fire, add them to the side so that the main heat is not dispersed. Or you could light a second batch of charcoal to use for topping up in a second barbecue or in an old metal drum or tin.

If you need to create a cool spot, heap the coals up more on one side than the other.

Gas-burning barbecues

Convenient and fast, gas barbecues can be fixed or portable and run on mains gas or LPG. They provide instant heat, which is easy to control – just like a gas ring in the kitchen. They're easy to clean and keep clean, unlike charcoal-burning barbecues, which get dirty and grimy after the first barbecue. Gas-burning barbecues are generally more economical than charcoal-burning barbecues, too.

Some come with all the bells and whistles – a wok attachment, gas burners on the side, a smoker, rotisserie, cupboards and drawers, a timer and temperature gauge, racks for hanging tools – everything bar the kitchen sink (some

really flash barbecues actually have a sink!). Most now come with a hood, and you can use them as you would an oven, especially for roasting large joints of meat. You don't get the smoky flavours that you do from a wood-fired or charcoal-burning barbecue, but you can create them to some extent by using lava rocks or ceramic bricks (see below).

The grill rack

Providing a fast heat source that lets food sear and sizzle with little added fat, a grill rack is responsible for creating a smoky flavour in food – the true barbecue taste! Meat should be trimmed of as much fat as possible because excess fat dripping onto the embers (or heat source) can flare up and burn the food.

Place a layer of pumice or sand or similar (we use clean cat litter at our house) on the drip tray underneath the grill rack to absorb fat and oil. Whatever you use, it will need regular changing. Clean the grill rack with a stiff wire brush kept specifically for the purpose – and hot soapy water if necessary.

When using a gas barbecue, grilling is best done in conjunction with either lava rocks, ceramic bricks or pumice laid out on a tray. The tray should sit on top of the gas burners, below the grill, so the heat can be spread, making it more even and providing a wider grill surface. As juices drip onto the hot rocks, they make smoke that flavours the food. The rocks should be turned over from time to time to let the drippings burn off, or washed according to the manufacturer's recommendation.

The hot plate

The hot plate is an invaluable part of a barbecue (be aware that not all barbecues come with a hot plate and you may need to buy one separately). It's a heavy, solid piece of metal on which food is seared and cooked. The food retains a little more fat or moisture than when cooked on the grill rack because it sits in oil or in its own juices (these drip off the grill rack, but on a hot plate they slowly pool to the sides and are funnelled to the drip tray).

Whether you cook on the grill rack or hot plate depends on the food to be barbecued. Sliced aubergine, brushed with oil, is best on the hot plate because it can go dry and rubbery over the dry heat of the grill rack. Steaks do well on either because generally they have a marbling of fat throughout, which helps keep them moist. Prawns in the shell can also be done on either, but have more flavour if done on the grill rack because the shells, which protect the delicate flesh, singe a little in the flames. Use the hot plate for delicate items such as fish cakes, which could crumble and fall through the grid of the grill rack. It's also good for small items such as slivers of garlic, pieces of pared lemon rind, and narrow fillets of fish that could slip through the grid. Think of the hot plate as a giant non-stick frying pan, on which you can sizzle bacon, make pancakes and crêpes, cook eggs over-easy or sunny-side-up, cook satay and steaks, chicken fillets and lamb cutlets – just about anything you fancy. Food can also be reheated on the hot plate – use a sturdy saucepan or a wok or frying pan, or place the food to be reheated in an aluminium foil pouch over a low to medium heat.

Food cooked on the hot plate will not necessarily have a smoky flavour, but some things, such as cutlets and steaks, can be put over the grill rack for the final moments of cooking. This will impart a hint of smoke and if you've got lava rocks in place, it's just about as good as the flavour you'd get from grilling from the start. Once you've transferred the food from the hot plate to the grill rack you should fan the heat source several times so that the flames gently lick the food at least once or twice.

You will quickly get to know your hot plate and how to judge the temperature, but here's a quick test: hold your hand 4–5cm above the source of heat. If it's uncomfortably hot after 2 seconds the hot plate is really hot; if it gets hot after 4 seconds, it's a medium heat; and if you can hold your hand there for 6 seconds or more, it's a low heat.

When and how

What you cook and how you cook it is not always the main motivation for cooking on a barbecue. Because you're cooking outside, all the splatters will fall on the grass, or onto bricks or concrete and subsequently get washed away in the rain or burnt off in the sun. It sure saves on housework!

Overloading the grill rack or hot plate should be avoided because it makes food difficult to turn, stops juices from evaporating and can make food steam instead of sear and sizzle. The correct cooking temperature is also vital. Most food is better cooked on medium heat or even cooler than that to start. Take sausages, for instance. Start them off slowly or they will quickly char and form a hard glazed skin that the heat will have trouble penetrating. Increase the heat during the cooking and at the end to finish browning.

Charred food is not healthy and while a little bit of charring adds an interesting hint of bitterness or caramel flavour, it is better to keep it to a minimum (however, charring red capsicums and aubergines is fine when they are going to be peeled before serving).

Always preheat the barbecue (10 minutes is all it should take to heat a gas barbecue – any longer and you may be wasting fuel or risking meltdown) unless you are cooking steaks, which require an even source of highish heat. It also pays to keep one part of the cooking area cooler than the rest so you can move food to a cooler part once it is done while waiting for other pieces to finish off.

Cooking meat

Resist the temptation to constantly move meat around. Leave it alone. Don't prod, poke, stir or turn unnecessarily. Food often sticks at the beginning of cooking, but frees itself quite nicely as the proteins start to cook. If you interfere with that and forcibly try to prise stuck meat off the hot plate, you'll tear the fibres, making it stringy, and ruin the surface of the meat.

Another disadvantage of moving meat around too much is that it will cool down and may lose its cooking momentum. If this happens it starts to get a bit stewy underneath – in other words it'll lose its sizzle. And if you prod and poke you're likely to pierce the meat and let out juices – what you're trying to do is to keep juices in the meat so that it will be nice and juicy when you come to eat it. Those fierce-looking barbecue forks with the pointy prongs should be banned from barbecues! It's hard to give exact cooking times for meats (see chart on page 151 for doneness) because it depends on the thickness of the hot plate or the heat from the embers and the wind or chill factor.

Cooking fish

Fish requires special attention because it cooks quickly on the barbecue and continues to cook as it stands. Therefore, remove fish from the grill or hot plate *before* it is totally cooked. By doing this, the fish will continue cooking from the residual heat and stay moist and succulent. When cooking fish fillets, it's better to cook one side well (i.e. until golden and good-looking) than sear the other side without cooking it through. Then, when serving it, present it with the good-looking side uppermost. If you cook both sides of a fillet until golden, in most cases the fish will be dried out and tough to eat.

Tools

• Tongs are essential – and long-handled tongs in particular can save you from singeing your skin; just make sure they are easy to use because some brands are rather cumbersome.

• In New Zealand you can buy a barbecue scraper called a Bar-B-Mate. It's every backyard barbecuer's favourite tool by a long shot, it's cleverly designed with a sharp edge that can be used to cut food and little pointy 'teeth' at one end that will hook pieces of food. It can also be used to release fat from food, as in the case of fatty sausages (simply use the pointy teeth to prick the food). A large paint scraper will do the job, but it doesn't have the same cachet.

• Invest in two good basting brushes with natural bristles or heatproof silicon bristles (nylon bristles will melt). Keep one for brushing oil or glazes over food, and a larger one for brushing the hot plate with oil.

• You'll also need a wire brush for scrubbing the grill rack and a device that can be used as a small fan to fan the flames when necessary.

• Have old tea towels on hand to wipe up spillages and to rub down the hot plate after it has been cleaned.

• If the barbecue doesn't have automatic ignition, buy long-handled matches or a long-handled lighter.

• Thick oven gloves or mitts are useful when working with a smoker or rotisserie.

• Keep a small bottle of water to spray on flare-ups or use a kid's water pistol (handy for pesky animals – or kids!).

• Fish grills are useful for cooking whole fish and fish fillets, especially when it's time to turn them.

Skewers

Metal skewers conduct heat and so are good for chunky food and thicker pieces of meat. Use bamboo skewers for vegetables, fish and for satay made with thin strips of meat. To prevent bamboo skewers from scorching at the ends, soak them in cold water for 30 minutes before use.

Rosemary stalks make excellent skewers as well as flavouring the food they are skewering. Choose firm stalks; remove most of the leaves other than a little cluster at the tip of each, then let them dry off and harden for a day. If you find it difficult to pierce the food with a rosemary stalk, use a pointed metal skewer to make the hole, then skewer with the rosemary stalk.

Lemon grass stalks can also be used and are particularly good with seafood and chicken.

Marinating

Never marinate food in copper, cast-iron or aluminium and preferably not in aluminium foil containers. This is because the acids (e.g. wine, tomatoes, lemons, etc) in the marinades can react with these metals, causing discolouration of the food or affecting flavour. American recipes may call for a non-reactive bowl for the marinade; in other words a bowl made of glass, china, ceramic or plastic that won't react with marinade ingredients.

Always scrape off marinades or spice pastes before putting food on the barbecue because they can burn. Any left-over marinade can be brushed over the food for the final few minutes of cooking.

Big joints of meat are more easily marinated by putting them in a sturdy sealable plastic bag to which you then add the marinade. Put the bag in a large bowl, in case of leakage, then turn the bag over and over until the joint is coated in marinade. There's no messy turning with spoons – all you need to do is turn the bag over from time to time as the contents marinate.

Tender meats and fish need hardly any marinating; they will actually lose texture and structure if left in an acidic marinade for too long (I once turned a bowl of squid rings to mush by marinating them overnight in sliced kiwifruit!).

Do not use marinade juices in a sauce or in a finished dish unless they have been boiled first. This is because they are likely to contain raw meat juices, which must be cooked to make them safe to eat.

Tips

• Ensure the gas tank is full before you start barbecuing.

• Have everything ready so that you don't need to dash back to the kitchen and leave the food unattended.

• Tie a clump of herbs (e.g. rosemary, thyme and a bay leaf) together, and use to brush marinades over meats and fish, imparting fragrance as you go.

• On a really windy day, barbecuing can be slow. Make an aluminium foil tent and place it over the food on the barbecue. By locking in some of the heat the food will cook more quickly.

• To impart a slight smoky flavour, put some soaked wood chips in a double thickness pouch of aluminium foil. Poke a few small holes in the foil with a skewer, then put the pouch on top of the burners underneath the grill rack and then cook the food on the grill rack.

• Use a piece of aluminium foil as a lid over foods that you want to steam – it saves on dishes.

• Remove silverskin and as much fat as possible from the meat before barbecuing it.

• If using a sweet glaze made with honey or sugar, brush it on for the last few minutes of cooking only, otherwise it may burn.

• Salt the meat *after* cooking (unless stated otherwise) because it can make the surface of the meat wet, which will cause spitting. It can also draw out the juices too early, especially when added to a marinade.

Time-savers

Chicken drumsticks take a long time to cook thoroughly on the barbecue. Speed up the process by slashing them once or twice to the bone with a sharp knife (this has the advantage of letting in the marinade, too). Chicken breasts can be butterflied (split open) for quicker cooking, and whole chickens spatchcocked (cut down the backbone and forced to lie flat by snapping the ball and socket joints of the thighs and wings). Boned chicken thighs will cook more quickly than thighs with the bone in. To speed up cooking sausages, split them in half down the length.

If using a disposable barbecue, remember that they are good for thinly sliced meats, bacon, browning cooked corn, satay made with thinly sliced meats, fish, burgers, cutlets and chops and the like; but not so reliable for dense-fleshed food or big joints of meat. Cool the barbecue completely before disposing of it.

Cleaning

It's much easier to clean a gas barbecue while it is still hot. The best way I know to clean it is to splash a cup of water onto the plate, then scrape it clean. Dry it off with a piece of towel kept for the purpose. Even burnt sugar or stuck-on gunk will come off this way.

Charcoal barbecues should be left until they are cold before being emptied. Ashes should be completely cold before you dispose of them.

Health

• Always wash your hands before barbecuing.

• All meats should be thoroughly defrosted before being cooked on the barbecue. Don't defrost meats in full sunlight; they are best thawed slowly in the refrigerator (overnight is usually sufficient).

• Marinate food in the fridge, unless it's for a very short period.

• Bring meats to room temperature before barbecuing them, but be aware that on a warm day even thick cuts of chicken need only 10–15 minutes after being taken from the fridge to come to room temperature.

• Don't leave raw meats sitting in the sun or in a warm spot too close to the barbecue.

• Always wash hands before and after handling raw poultry or meats.

• Do not use the same chopping board for raw and cooked meats.

• Don't mix raw fish and raw meats – keep them separate.

• Never serve cooked meats on the same dish or tray on which they sat when raw. A good trick is to line the tray or dish with a double thickness of plastic food wrap, removing it only once the meat is put on the barbecue thereby creating a clean surface to put the cooked meat on.

• If using a temperature probe, wash it between insertions. If

you insert it into raw poultry, then leave it hanging around in a warm spot before reinserting it into cooked poultry, you risk spreading bacteria.

• It's important that mince is thoroughly cooked. Buy freshly minced meat and use it as soon after purchase as possible.

• Watch out for family pets – keep all meats covered and out of their reach.

• Use an outdoor chilly, esky or polystyrene bin filled with ice packs to keep food chilled outdoors.

Safety
• Discourage children from playing around a barbecue; in fact it's best to establish a no-go area around the barbecue and food preparation area.

• Have a small fire extinguisher handy or, failing that, a bucket of water, sand or earth in case you need it to throw over the fire if it gets out of control.

• Open the lid of a gas barbecue before lighting it.

• Don't attempt to move the barbecue once it is lit.

• Disposable and portable barbecues should be placed on an even heatproof surface such as bricks or paving stones.

• Flare-ups are caused by a small amount of fat, oil or marinade dripping onto the fire. The flames can blacken food and make it taste bitter. Douse the flames with a squirt of water.

Extras
Open-air cooking and eating should be incident-free so everyone can enjoy themselves.

While barbecuing in the dark with the rain pouring down and the only light coming from a candle or a miner's hat can be done, it's no fun. A good overhead light that shines onto the hot plate or grill is a real asset as is protection from the elements (preferably via see-through material that doesn't block natural light).

Provide plenty of paper serviettes and rolls of absorbent kitchen paper. A bin lined with a plastic bag will make tidying up quick and easy.

Finger bowls are helpful when serving mussels or prawns in the shell or sticky satay.

Cast-iron grill pan

For those times when you want grilled food, but it's raining cats and dogs so you just can't face the barbecue, I suggest you invest in a ridged cast-iron grill pan. With one of these you'll be able to cook steaks, shellfish and vegetables, albeit in small quantities at a time, indoors out of the rain.

Preheat the pan over a medium heat. Oil the food, not the pan. Once you have put the food in the hot pan, don't attempt to move it until it has been cooking for some time. This is because it will stick to the pan in the beginning; don't worry, this is normal. Brown one side of the food to a good golden colour. Turn and cook on the second side just enough to sear (to avoid overcooking). Serve it golden side up.

Leave the pan to cool before soaking it in water, then wash it by hand. Cast-iron pans should not be washed with soap. Dry it thoroughly then rub with a little oil to prevent rusting.

Steak talk

• Buy quality meat – cheap meat will make a cheap eat and you'll feel cheated at the end of it.

• Steaks should not be cut too thin because they can shrivel or curl, and it is difficult to get them nicely browned without overcooking them.

• Have meat at room temperature before putting it on the barbecue so that it starts cooking evenly as soon as it hits the grill.

• Don't press down on steaks while they cook as this will squeeze out juices.

• Salt meat *after* cooking as salt draws out moisture and makes meat spit when it hits hot oil, and causes it to lose juices.

• Let steaks rest for 5 minutes before serving. This allows the meat to reabsorb its juices, making it more succulent in the mouth.

• While the above tips will help, my top tip is to get to know a butcher near you. Find the best one in your area and tell them what you want, and what you expect of a fresh meat supplier. You need to give them your business, but you may need to guide them. If you don't give them your business, much like the fruiterer and fishmonger in so many towns they'll disappear down the gurgler.

Touch test for cooked beef

To check cooked meat for doneness, press with tongs:
- very rare beef 'gives' under pressure, feels very soft to the touch
- rare beef feels soft to the touch
- medium–rare beef feels soft and springy to the touch
- medium beef feels firm and springy to the touch
- well done beef feels firm to the touch
- very well done beef feels very firm to the touch.

Sausage stuff

Picking the right porker, or beef, chicken, lamb, venison or any other type of sausage, is crucial. Little joy is to be had from mass-produced sausages full of extenders and cereals, or from precooked tubes of solidified gloop that look as if they have been piped on the mortuary slab.

Good sausages will cost you more. So be it. Think of them as a good meal rather than something to throw on the barbie to fill in the gaps, with leftovers going to the dog. Would you throw leftover pieces of fillet steak to the dog? Probably not. It's more likely you'd keep them for sandwiches or a salad. A good sausage should similarly be respected not least because leftover sausages are good tucker. Just remember to put them away in the fridge as soon as possible after cooking.

The word 'sausage' can be traced back to its Latin roots, *salsus*, which means salted. Basically, it was a way of preserving meat, especially all the unmentionable bits after a pig was slaughtered. Some sausages would be air-dried, others were smoked. We've been eating them since time immemorial. Germany has over 1000 types of sausage, but Italy produces the biggest. Baby mortadella sausages (an aromatic and spicy pork sausage) weigh as little as half a kilo, but the big mammas can weigh over 100kg. They take their sausages seriously in Europe. I wish we did the same here.

Snarlers or snags, or whatever else you may call them, sausages have been the butt of too many jokes and have been unfairly incinerated too many times. Chosen with care and cooked with attention, they are the quintessential barbecue food, perfect for any situation or occasion, and pleasing to everyone. Quality vegetarian sausages can be found at specialist butchers.

Finally, barbecuing should be fun. The high adventure of the spit and sizzle ... the chit-chat and laughter ... glass of wine in hand ... maybe even the rumble of surf in the background ... with food so good, barbecuing begs to be repeated for as long as the weather continues to favour you.

glossary

Ancho chilli
A dried poblano chilli, brick red to mahogany in colour, with a sweet, mild and fruity flavour. Ancho are usually toasted to develop the flavour and then soaked to soften before use.

Aubergine (eggplant)
There's no need to salt aubergines unless there is a lot of green immediately under the skin (the greenness indicates immaturity, which may make the aubergine taste bitter). In this case slice or cut aubergine as directed, then place layers in a colander sprinkling each layer with salt. Put a plate under the colander and leave aubergine to drain for 30 minutes, then pat dry with absorbent kitchen paper and carry on with the recipe.

Baguette
This long stick of crusty bread is also known as French bread or a French stick.

Balsamic vinegar
This superior vinegar, a specialty of Modena in Italy, is made using a centuries-old technique. The juice of trebbiano grapes is boiled down to a syrup, then poured into wooden barrels where it is left for at least five years, in some cases much longer. The resulting vinegar is aromatic, spicy and sweet-sour to taste and should be used sparingly. Most of the cheap balsamic vinegars contain caramel, not grape syrup.

Banana leaves
Banana leaves can be used as a plate on which to serve barbecued food (wash and shake dry first). If the middle rib is removed the leaves can be shaped into cones and used as food containers. Pass the banana leaves over a flame to soften them and make them flexible, or blanch in boiling water for a few seconds. The softened leaves can also be used as wrappers for fish, vegetables and meats. Use natural string to tie the parcels.

Besan
Ground from a type of chick pea, this flour is used as a thickener, in batters, and as a flavouring. It's also known as channa flour.

Bird's eye chillies
These small, hot chilli peppers with a fruity, plummy flavour provide a tingle on the tongue when used in moderation, and an explosive fiery heat when used generously. Dried bird's eye chillies are stipulated throughout this book. Use whole or crushed, as directed.

Bruschetta
Toasted bread (preferably ciabatta or thick-crusted textural bread) rubbed with garlic and doused with extra virgin olive oil.

Butterflied leg of lamb
To butterfly a leg of lamb, remove the bone and trim away excess fat. A good butcher will butterfly a leg of lamb for you at no cost. The lamb can then be seasoned, rolled and tied before roasting, or cooked flat on the barbecue.

Buttermilk
The term buttermilk was used to describe the liquid residue of milk or cream after it was churned to make butter. These days 'cultured' buttermilk is made by adding a natural culture to standard milk or skimmed milk. The addition of buttermilk makes baked items (e.g. scones) lighter, as well as adding a slight tang.

Capers, salted
Capers are the unopened flower buds of a Mediterranean shrub. Picked while still tightly clenched, they are dried in the sun, then layered in barrels with rock salt or with vinegar. It is this process which enhances their flavour. Capers packed in salt have a more authentic caper flavour than those packed in vinegar or brine. Check that the salt is white, not yellowing (an indication of age). Wash off loose salt before using and soak the capers in several changes of warm water until they lose any excessive salty taste. If using capers in brine, drain them well, rinse under running water and leave to drain again before using.

Chicken fillet (tenderloin)
This is the long, thin pointy strip of tender meat that can easily be separated from the breast itself. Use sliced chicken breast as a substitute.

Chorizo sausages
A Spanish pork sausage flavoured with paprika and garlic of varying degrees of hotness. Fresh, soft chorizo sausages need to

be cooked, but dried versions can be served in the same way as salami, or sliced and fried and served hot as tapas.

Ciabatta

Italian in origin, ciabatta is a slipper-shaped flattish loaf of bread with a holey texture, a distinctive sour taste and a thin, chewy crust. Use it fresh, rebake it until crisp, or use for bruschetta.

Coconut cream, canned

A thick form of coconut milk that separates in the can into two distinct components: a rich cream and a watery liquid. Either scoop off the rich cream from the top and use as directed in curries, sauces or desserts (the watery liquid is good to use in soups, curries or baking, or to cook rice) or shake the can to get a smooth milk.

Couscous, instant

The little dried semolina pellets, which constitute instant couscous, can be quickly softened in hot water or stock and served in place of rice or potatoes.

Craisins

Craisins are dried cranberries that have been halved and then sweetened to make them palatable (fresh cranberries are too astringent to eat without sugar). Known as a nutrient-dense fruit, rich in antioxidants and flavonoids, they're a proven preventative of urinary tract infections. Craisins contain all the goodness of cranberries. Nibble on them as you would raisins or dried fruit; add to fresh and dried fruit salads; use in stuffings for turkey, chicken, duck and quail; or add to muffins and fruit loaves.

Creamy Dijon mustard

A rich and creamy mustard flecked with crushed mustard seeds, use this as you would Dijon mustard (although you can be more generous with it because it is quite mild). It's particularly good in dressings because it helps to thicken and emulsify.

Cumin seeds, toasted

Toasting cumin seeds gives them a rich earthy aroma and flavour. Put the seeds in a small, dry frying pan and set it over a medium heat. Toast the seeds for a few minutes, shaking the pan occasionally until they start popping, darken in colour and smell fragrant. Grind the seeds in a spice grinder, or pulverise them with a mortar and pestle. Toast more than you need and store the remainder in an airtight jar once cool.

Demerara sugar

These hard light-brown crystals with a mild caramel flavour get their name from Demerara, Guyana. They are especially good to use for forming a crunchy topping on baking.

Dried oregano, Sicilian and Greek

A particularly sweet and fragrant form of oregano which becomes more potent once it is dried, it should be stored in a container away from light. Before using, rub it between the palms of your hands to release its fragrance.

Dukkah

A ground mixture of fragrant spices and nuts which can be used as a dunk with bread and oil, as well as a flavouring in and on things, or stirred into yoghurt and served as a sauce.

Fish sauce

A thin pungent sauce made from salted fermented fish, which (although it sounds revolting) is the key flavouring in many Asian dishes. It works by seasoning the food rather than imparting a fishy flavour.

Ginger

When ginger is very young and fresh, it has the texture of a crisp apple and doesn't need peeling; at this stage it is milder in flavour and can be used liberally. Look for plump, firm clumps of ginger (called hands), avoiding any that are withered, as they will be pungent and coarsely textured. The best way to store ginger is to wrap it in absorbent kitchen paper and keep it in the vegetable crisper. This prevents it from getting moist and then rotting (it will eventually shrivel). It can also be kept in the freezer in a zip-lock bag and grated from the frozen state, and it can be immersed in a jar of sherry, providing an aromatic liquid to add to Chinese-inspired dishes.

Greek yoghurt

This thick and creamy yoghurt is usually made from sheep's milk. If not available, place the required amount of natural yoghurt in a sieve lined with a piece of absorbent kitchen paper. Drain for 30–60 minutes before carefully turning out into a bowl, and peeling off the paper.

Haloumi

Sometimes spelled haloumy, in Cyprus this salty sheep's milk cheese is flavoured with dried mint and in Lebanon with black cumin seed. It is squeaky and rubbery when raw, and meltingly tender when heated.

Kaffir lime leaves

The fresh leaves of the makrut lime tree are wonderfully fragrant, smelling somewhat sweeter than lime zest, and fresh and citrusy clean. They can be rolled and sliced exceedingly thin (it's best to remove the leaf stem first), and added to uncooked dishes, or the double-leafed leaf (shaped like two arrowheads pointing in opposite directions) can be added whole to curries, stuffed inside fish or floated in soups. Dried leaves are a poor substitute; use lime zest or lemon zest instead.

Kecap manis
Also known as ketjap manis, this Indonesian thick and sweet soy sauce – made from soya beans, palm sugar and spices including star anise – is available from Asian food stores. Refrigerate after opening.

Kumara
Kumara are sweet potatoes. They make a great mash and can be used successfully in soups and salads, pies and quiches. They also roast well and make great fries. Kumara can be baked in their jackets or skins, which are particularly nutritious.

Lamb shortloin
This boneless lean piece of meat (about 20cm long and weighing around 200g) is cut from the middle loin and is obtained by removing the rack and cutting between the twelfth and thirteenth ribs. It is also known as lamb backstrap.

Lamb tenderloins
Like the eye fillet of beef, this piece is the tenderest of all the lamb cuts. It's a small lean strip, 2–3cm thick, about 20cm long (once trimmed) with the grain running lengthways. Remove the silverskin before using. Allow 2 per person, and cook for 2–3 minutes only.

Lemon- and mandarin-infused olive oil
These extra virgin olive oils infused with citrus essences are reasonably easy to source but if not available, use extra virgin olive oil to which has been added a little finely grated zest and juice of an orange or lemon.

Mango cheeks
This term refers to the fleshy 'cheeks' on each side of the large, flat mango seed.

Manuka honey
The honey made from the flowers of the manuka tree (native to New Zealand) possesses an earthy, oily, herbaceous aroma and flavour. Rich, dark and intense, it has antibacterial and anti-fungal properties. As a substitute use an intensely flavoured thick honey.

Minced meat
Minced meat quickly loses its freshness due to its preparation and exposure to air. Buy freshly minced meat and use on day of purchase or soon after. Cook thoroughly.

Mortadella
A specialty sausage from Bologna traditionally made from pure pork, it has a captivating aroma and a mild spicy, savoury flavour. Available in sizes from 500g up to a giant sausage weighing 100kg!

Mozzarella, bocconcini
Traditionally, mozzarella was made from buffalo's milk, but it is now usually made from cow's milk and sold as a fresh cheese or vacuum-packed in whey. Bocconcini is the Italian name for small bite-sized balls of mozzarella.

Mozzarella, buffalo
Mozzarella cheese made from buffalo's milk is softer and creamier than cow's milk mozzarella, with a high moisture content and a delicate sweet milky-earthy flavour. It melts more easily than cow's milk mozzarella.

Olives, queen
These large green olives originate in Spain. With their meaty texture and sweet and mildly briny flavour, they're good for using in cooked dishes and on kebabs as they hold together.

Parmesan cheese
Authentic parmesan cheese (Parmigiano-Reggiano) has an intoxicating aroma and a spicy flavour with an interesting granular texture. Parmesan lookalikes tend to be highly seasoned, soapy, dry, coarse-textured or inferior in some way. Real parmesan melts without running, browns well, isn't greasy and doesn't become rubbery. It is quickly digested (even by infants) and low in calories. Buy it in the piece, keep it treble-wrapped in aluminium foil and store it in the door or the coolest part of the fridge. If storing for a long period, change the foil every so often and wipe the rind clean. Grate parmesan as required, because it quickly loses its aroma and flavour.

Parsley
All parsley used in the recipes in this book is of the flat-leafed variety, often called Italian parsley. It has a fresh, grassy flavour. Regular parsley can be substituted if it's not available.

Pide
This long thin and soft Turkish bread can be toasted or crisped in the oven, split and filled.

Pine nuts
Pine nuts are the seeds of the stone pine. Small and creamy coloured, when the nuts are fresh they smell sweet and aromatic and have a nutty creamy taste. More expensive than other nuts because they are difficult to harvest, they require a period of drying during which time the cones ripen and reveal the nuts

within. Use pine nuts whole in sweet and savoury dishes. Pine nuts turn rancid quite quickly; buy them in small quantities and store in a container in the freezer.

Polenta
Polenta is a type of porridge, usually made from ground corn, which is cooked by slowly adding it to boiling liquid, usually water or sometimes milk, and cooking until it thickens. It can be served as is, with butter and cheese, or topped with a meaty sauce or stew, or cooled and cut into shapes and fried, grilled or baked. In the Vento region of Italy you'll find a white polenta which has a milder corn flavour. It is often sold pre-boiled, in a slab, ready to fry, grill or bake. Polenta can also be made from buckwheat, a specialty of Treviso, Italy. It remains a staple food in the north of Italy and it's also popular in Tuscany. It is standard fare in most Balkan countries, too.

Polenta, instant
Regular polenta gives off a pronounced corn aroma as it cooks and has a richer corn taste and 'gruntier' texture than instant polenta, but most people will find these differences hard to detect. If you're a purist use regular polenta, which will take around 25 minutes to cook. But if you're a speedy cook, opt for the instant variety – it will cook in about 5 minutes.

Potatoes
Potatoes are either waxy or floury, but some potatoes are less waxy or less floury than others and are known as all-purpose potatoes. All-purpose potatoes do most jobs well, but may not shine at any particular one.

Waxy potatoes
Waxy describes the texture of the potato. New potatoes are waxy because their sugar has not yet converted to starch, as it will with age. Waxy potatoes are good for salads because the potato holds together after slicing or dicing. And if you want to add potatoes to a casserole, use waxy ones because they will hold their shape.
Examples: most freshly-dug spring potatoes such as Jersey bennes, early season desiree, early season Duke of York, draga, concorde, maris anchor, nicola, kipfler.

Floury potatoes
Floury describes the texture of the potato. A floury potato is low in moisture and sugar and high in starch. Floury potatoes are excellent for mashing and for roasting and cooking in embers. They also make good chips and wedges. Use floury potatoes to thicken soups because they will dissolve in the soup and thicken the liquid. Examples: agria, rua, Dakota, russet Burbank, desiree, sebago, King Edward.

Poussin
This is the French term for a baby chicken weighing around 450–500g.

Prosciutto
Sometimes referred to as Parma ham, this is sold either as prosciutto crudo, a raw ham cured by air and salt (not, as is often presumed, by smoking) or prosciutto cotto, a cooked version. In this book, prosciutto refers to the raw, cured ham. It is sliced very thin with a strip of sweet-tasting fat attached (the fat is part of the experience, giving the cured meat a softer edge). It can be served as an antipasto component, used to wrap around food, or added to stuffings and pasta sauces.

Refreshing
This means to rinse with water. Vegetables are refreshed with a cup or two of cold water after blanching or cooking for any of the following reasons: to halt the cooking process, to remove strong flavours, or to help keep the colour. When refreshing pasta or rice, use warm water, as cold makes the starch tacky.

Salt
Salt is the most indispensable ingredient in the kitchen. It draws out nuances of flavour which, had the food been left unsalted, may have lain dormant. Compensating for not using salt in the cooking by sprinkling it on the cooked food is not the same – you are likely to taste only salt.

Sambal oelek
Made from pounded chillies, salt and vinegar or tamarind, a sambal (meaning relish or sauce) is used to spice up dishes. Sometimes spelled sambal ulek or sambal olek, it is available as a pre-prepared condiment.

Sea salt
Comprising small crystalline flakes of salt, a good sea salt is completely natural, has no additives or bitter aftertaste and has a less aggressive taste than common table salt. Sea salt flakes are easily crumbled and dissolve in dressings and sauces (rock salt is much harder and should not be used on top of baked items, such as bread, because it becomes hard enough to crack teeth – it's good for quickly salting a large saucepan of boiling water).

Shallots, crisp fried
You can cook sliced shallots gently for 30–40 minutes until crisp or buy them ready-made from Asian food stores. Sprinkle them over dishes or add to peanut sauces or condiments. They're wonderfully sweet and mildly pungent.

Shallots, fresh

These small clusters of bulbs that grow like garlic have a mild onion flavour and can be used raw, or fried or roasted. As their size varies greatly, in this book I have specified a cup quantity of sliced shallots (e.g. ½ cup), rather than a quantity of bulbs.

Sherry vinegar

Sherry vinegar, from Jerez de la Frontera in Spain, is made by the traditional ageing method used for making fine wines and sherry (which involves aging it for at least six months, and sometimes for years). It's sharp and refreshing, with hints of oak and caramel. Use sparingly in sauces, gravies and stuffings, or splashed over vegetables and meats.

Splatter screen

This useful round fine-wire mesh screen can be placed over a frying pan while food is frying. It lets air come and go but confines most of the splatters to within the pan – and it's dishwasher proof.

Sugar, granulated

Granulated sugar is just another way to describe regular white sugar (the sort you serve with tea). It's used in syrups because it produces a clearer result than the more 'dusty' caster sugar, which can produce a cloudy syrup. Caster sugar is finer and is used in baking because it is easier to cream with butter or mix with other ingredients.

Sugar, palm

Palm sugar is made from the sap extracted from young palms, boiled down to a syrup. It has an intense, sweet caramel-like flavour. Grate or chop before use. Store any leftover palm sugar in an airtight container.

Tahini

This thick, oily paste made from toasted sesame seeds is also known as tahina. Mix with yoghurt and garlic or with cooked, mashed aubergine and garlic to make a delicious dip.

Thai basil

Thai basil (horapa) has a subtle, sweet licorice flavour, quite different to the deeply aromatic herb associated with Italian cooking, and is used to flavour curries, soups and salads.

Tomatoes, canned

Tomatoes need lots of sun to develop their full, sweet flavour. Italian canned tomatoes generally have a vibrant orangey-red colour, a meaty texture with few seeds, thick (not watery) juice, and a sweet, fruity taste that tastes as if they've been packed in sunshine.

Tomatoes, green

Unripe green tomatoes are crisp and fruity tasting and have quite an acidic bite. They can be floured or crumbed and fried, or used in salads. You'll need to order them from your greengrocer.

Tomatoes, Roma

These oval-shaped fleshy tomatoes are good for sauce because they have more flesh than water. They're also good for slow-roasting.

Tomatoes, skinning

When tomatoes are eaten fresh, as in a salad, there is usually no need to remove the skins unless they are tough. But if the tomatoes are to be used in soups, sauces or vegetable stews, it is advisable to do so. The skin tends to separate from the flesh during cooking and float to the surface. It has a tough texture and looks unappetising. Another reason to discard them is because cooked tomato skins are not easily digested. The skins can be removed by immersing the tomato in hot water so it swells, making the skin taut and causing it to burst. Do this by dropping the tomatoes into a saucepan of boiling water and leave for 12–20 seconds, depending on how ripe they are. Lift out the tomatoes with a slotted spoon and transfer to a bowl of cold water. If a tomato is difficult to peel, repeat the process. If the tomato looks fluffy or furry, it was in the water for too long and has started to cook; reduce the time for any further tomatoes.

Tomatoes, vine-ripened

Tomatoes ripened on the vine have much more flavour than those grown indoors. Use them in salads.

Vanilla extract

Vanilla essence is a cheap imitation form of vanilla. Look for vanilla extract, which is made from real vanilla.

Verjuice

Verjuice, made from unripened white grapes, is used as an acidulant in much the same way vinegar and lemon juice are used, although it is milder than both. Use verjuice to deglaze pans and roasting dishes, or add it to vinaigrettes and sauces. Refrigerate once opened.

weights & measures

Grams to Ounces and vice versa

GENERAL			EXACT		
30g	=	1oz	1oz	=	28.35g
60g	=	2oz	2oz	=	56.70g
90g	=	3oz	3oz	=	85.05g
120g	=	4oz	4oz	=	113.04g
150g	=	5oz	5oz	=	141.08g
180g	=	6oz	6oz	=	170.01g
210g	=	7oz	7oz	=	198.04g
230g	=	8oz	8oz	=	226.08g
260g	=	9oz	9oz	=	255.01g
290g	=	10oz	10oz	=	283.05g
320g	=	11oz	11oz	=	311.08g
350g	=	12oz	12oz	=	340.02g
380g	=	13oz	13oz	=	368.05g
410g	=	14oz	14oz	=	396.09g
440g	=	15oz	15oz	=	425.02g
470g	=	16oz	16oz	=	453.06g

Recipes based on these (International Units) rounded values

Liquid Measurements

25ml	(28.4ml)	=	1fl oz				
150ml	(142ml)	=	5fl oz	=	¼ pint	=	1 gill
275ml	(284ml)	=	10fl oz	=	½ pint		
425ml	(426ml)	=	15fl oz	=	¾ pint		
575ml	(568ml)	=	20fl oz	=	1 pint		

Spoon Measures

¼ teaspoon	=	1.25ml
½ teaspoon	=	2.5ml
1 teaspoon	=	5ml
1 tablespoon	=	15ml

In NZ, SA, USA and UK 1 tablespoon = 15ml
In Australia 1 tablespoon = 20ml
1 tablespoon butter = 14g

For cup measures use a standard 250ml measuring cup

Measurements

cm to approx inches

0.5cm	=	¼ in	5cm	=	2 in
1.25cm	=	½ in	7.5cm	=	3 in
2.5cm	=	1 in	10cm	=	4 in

Oven Temperatures

CELSIUS	FAHRENHEIT	GAS	
110°C	225°F	¼	very cool
120°C	250°F	½	
140°C	275°F	1	cool
150°C	300°F	2	
170°C	325°F	3	moderate
180°C	350°F	4	
190°C	375°F	5	moderately hot
200°C	400°F	6	
220°C	425°F	7	hot
230°C	450°F	8	
240°C	475°F	9	very hot

Abbreviations

g	gram
kg	kilogram
mm	millimetre
cm	centimetre
ml	millilitre
tsp	teaspoon
Tbsp	tablespoon
°C	degrees Celsius
°F	degrees Fahrenheit

American-Imperial

in	inch
lb	pound
oz	ounce

index